A Strategist in Exile

Xenophon and the
Death of Thucydides

Rainer Nickel

Pen & Sword
MILITARY

First published in Great Britain in 2016 by
Pen & Sword Military
an imprint of
Pen & Sword Books Ltd
47 Church Street
Barnsley
South Yorkshire
S70 2AS

ISBN 978 1 47384 699 9

A CIP catalogue record for this book is available from the British
Library

Typeset in Minion by
Mac Style Ltd, Bridlington, East Yorkshire
Printed and bound in the UK by CPI Group (UK) Ltd,
Croydon, CRO 4YY

Pen & Sword Books Ltd incorporates the imprints of Pen & Sword
Archaeology, Atlas, Aviation, Battleground, Discovery, Family
History, History, Maritime, Military, Naval, Politics, Railways,
Select, Transport, True Crime, and Fiction, Frontline Books, Leo
Cooper, Praetorian Press, Seaforth Publishing and Wharncliffe.

For a complete list of Pen & Sword titles please contact
PEN & SWORD BOOKS LIMITED
47 Church Street, Barnsley, South Yorkshire, S70 2AS, England
E-mail: enquiries@pen-and-sword.co.uk
Website: www.pen-and-sword.co.uk

© Original Edition
„Der verbannte Stratege. Xenophon und der Tod des Thukydides", 2014
by Philipp von Zabern,
an imprint of WBG (Wissenschaftliche Buchgesellschaft), Darmstadt, Germany.

Contents

Introduction

Thucydides was the chronicler of the almost 30-year long Peloponnesian war, which came to a close with Sparta's victory over Athens in 404 BC. His famous historical work was preserved, but ends abruptly many years before the end of the war. It was continued decades later by Xenophon, with his 'Greek history' *Hellenica*.

Besides Thucydides' monograph on the Peloponnesian war and Xenophon's *Hellenica*, the most important source of the above portrayal is the war diary Xenophon published under the title *Anabasis*.

The people concerned are historical. A few secondary characters are created based upon these historical figures, but they should be quite true-to-life. Even the speeches and discussions described by Xenophon in his fictional memories are based on historical fact, and seek to follow established lore. The already ancient historian makes use of this medium of presentation to illustrate his historiographical positions and reflections, and to explain the actions of those concerned. The connection and meshing of plausible constructions and fictional recollections with historical fact is a tradition that reaches back into antiquity. Even today, this concept can allow people access to history which was previously unknown, if not completely alien.[1]

It is not, however, meant as a virtual history speculating on what may have happened had the principal players acted differently than they did in real life. Rather, the focus is on evidence-based reconstructions of situations in which the actual events may have played out. From the information passed down, a coherent narrative is woven. Gaps or voids in the sources are filled with the help of a controlled imagination, and reliable information is linked with the fictional narrative. Thus the motives for historical action – even where it cannot be verified that they have been passed down – become clear.[2]

The narrative is presented alternately as historical and fictionalised [in italics]. The Thirty Tyrants, who took power in Athens under the protection of the victor of the Peloponnesian war in 404 BC, allowed Thucydides to return from exile in Thrace. There will be a meeting between Xenophon and Thucydides. Xenophon's father invites the historian to his estate, but Thucydides vanishes without a trace shortly thereafter. Xenophon sets out to search for him – not only because they had become friends, but because he feels obliged to protect Thucydides from the Thirty Tyrants' regime of terror as far as he is able.[3] In addition, Thucydides had entrusted him with important historical documents he wanted to protect from destruction. But Thucydides remains untraceable.

It is thus most fortuitous that Xenophon is invited on a journey to Persia by his friend Proxenus in 401 BC. In reality, however, this 'journey' is the beginning of a military adventure, for which Cyrus – the younger brother of Artaxerxes, the Great King of Persia – had enlisted numerous Greek mercenaries, including Proxenus. Xenophon unwittingly accepts the invitation, hoping to make contact with the infamous Persian intelligence agency and intensify his search for Thucydides.

Only gradually does Xenophon learn that he has become embroiled in a dangerous conspiracy against Artaxerxes. But he cannot and will not go back. Then Cyrus gives him the honourable task of maintaining a war diary.

Finally, near Babylon, there is a pitched battle against the forces of the Great King. Cyrus falls. The rebellion has failed. The Greek mercenary army – numbering almost ten thousand men – remains, unbeaten, and refuses to submit to the Persian king. The Greek officers are lured into a trap: as they move into the Persian camp to negotiate their withdrawal, they are betrayed and murdered. Xenophon takes the initiative in the leaderless army and, surprisingly, he is selected to succeed Proxenus. He finally succeeds, under constant enemy threat and after overcoming tremendous hardship, in leading the men to the Black Sea and to safety.

It is not, however, recorded in history that Xenophon's participation in the march of the Ten Thousand was motivated by his search for Thucydides. It is as fictitious as his attempt to guard the historian against the Thirty. That he was trying to make up for his collaboration with the Thirty's regime of terror with his dedication to Thucydides, while reasonable, is not proven by the sources. It is a 'reconstruction of a possible history'.[4]

Though his search for Thucydides ultimately fails, Xenophon finally manages to find him in another way. The war diary confirms the historian's pessimistic evaluation of human behaviour,[5] won from his experiences in the Peloponnesian war. The *Anabasis* puts Thucydides' historical scheme of interpretation at centre stage – even if only on a relatively small and manageable one. The *Anabasis* portrays a panorama of failure, as well as the work of Thukydides: Cyrus' attempt, with the help of Greek mercenaries, to seize the throne of Persia fails, and even Xenophon's search for the missing Thucydides remains, despite everything, unsuccessful.

This panorama is enhanced with the portraits of important contemporaries: Socrates and the sophists, the historian Herodotus, the politicians Pericles, Cleon, Critias, Theramenes and Alcibiades, and even the comic playwright Aristophanes all play a part, among others. On an idealised historical stage, the famous friezes of the Parthenon of the Acropolis of Athens are briefly described: Xenophon 'recalls' how he gazed upon these friezes for the first time with his father during a cease-fire in the middle of the Peloponnesian war.

Traditional literary themes and motifs associated with specific places serve to enliven the narrative. In Ephesus, for example, Xenophon reminisces about the famous 'widow', and Sardis gives him the opportunity to describe an episode from the life of Croesus, the last Lydian king. In Celaenae, Xenophon makes mention of the Marsyas, who lost a musical competition with the god Apollo. These essays are, if nothing else, at least small examples of the linking of historical fact and literary fiction – they broaden the field of view.

Overview

The Story

The Peace Treaty

I*t is a cool spring morning. Around a hundred men stand on the battlements with hatchets and crowbars. Down the street, a handful of girls and women has gathered: flautists with their instruments. The Spartans had taken them from the bordellos and the dives before dawn. A bugle sounds. Drum roll. The musicians start the first song of a long day.[6] Rocks fall. Dust swirls. Sand and earth trickles. Aghast, the Athenians are forced to watch the destruction of the mighty structure.*

The sensible ones in the audience believe they are seeing the first day of freedom for the entirety of Hellas.[7] They are happy to have survived the devastating consequences of excessive, failed power politics.

With the destruction of the Long Walls, Athens fulfils the first part of the peace terms dictated by the Lacedaemonians after the devastating defeat in the Peloponnesian war. Xenophon replicates the wording exactly in his 'Greek history', the *Hellenica*:[8] 'The Lacedaemonians declare themselves willing to make peace under the following conditions: the Athenians must destroy the Long Walls and the fortifications of Piraeus. Surrender all ships except twelve, and allow your exiles to return. You count the same people among your friends and enemies as the Lacedaemonians, and follow them both by land and by sea wherever they should lead the way.'

The peace agreement was preceded by weeks of drama.[9] The Spartan commander, Lysander,[10] occupied the city of Lampsacus. Soon after, Byzantium and Chalcedon surrendered without struggle. The occupying Athenian troops were allowed to withdraw peacefully. Lysander sent the Athenian soldiers who had surrendered to him, and all others he had picked up along the way, back to Athens. They also granted safe conduct. In this way, Lysander wanted to finally defeat Sparta's rivals – he expected that the supply situation in the enclosed city would deteriorate quickly if they accepted refugees.

In Athens, fear of the Lacedaemonians grew every day. They were afraid that they would suffer what they themselves would have done to their defeated opponents in their unbridled arrogance. They prepared themselves for a long siege.

Lacedaemonian warships already blocked the Piraeus, and the Lacedaemonians began with a large-scale attack on the city by land, which was now completely cut off from the outside world and surrounded. Yet the Athenians were not yet ready to give in. Many people had already starved. Only when the situation became unbearable did the Athenians decide to contact Agis, the Spartan commander of the army blockade. They were, however, still unwilling to accept the Spartans' conditions and destroy the Long Walls and harbour fortifications. Negotiations were called off and delayed for months, but with the pressure of the catastrophic conditions in the city, the Athenians, finally, could see no other way out. They were at last ready to surrender unconditionally.

Among the opponent's allies, there were those who called for Athens to be completely destroyed. Luckily, the Lacedaemonians refused these demands, issued mainly by the Corinthians and Thebans: the Lacedaemonians were not prepared to raze to the ground a Hellenic city which had once accomplished great feats when Persians invaded Greece, and brought Hellas to the brink of disaster.[11]

The Rise of the Thirty

The fall of the Long Walls[12] marked the end of the Peloponnesian war. The mandated flute music that accompanied their destruction was to humiliate the vanquished opponent, who had once sacrificed to build the walls as an insurmountable barrier.

Key opponents of Athens' radical democracy had been working on a coup during the siege. Theramenes had played a special role in thwarting the surrender negotiations with Sparta. Achieving a better bargaining position with the Spartans was out of the question for him – he would rather bring his own people to their knees with hunger to eliminate his political opponents and to create an aristocratic regiment. He took advantage of the opportunity and overthrew the democratic government with the help of the Lacedaemonian commander. With pressure from the Spartans mounting, the remaining members of the ecclesia convened a commission of thirty men whom they regarded as more-or-less moderate opponents of democracy, and who would restore the old ways and thus restore order to the polis.

Xenophon later mentions this process in his *Hellenica*:[13] 'It was voted by the people to choose thirty men to put the laws of our fathers back into power, and to lead the polis in the spirit of these laws.'

Of course, the oligarchs laid out the provisions of the peace treaty in their own favour. 'Under pressure from Lysander's fleet, Athenian democracy was buried in midsummer of 404 BC. [...] After the oligarchs initially set up an 'action committee' of five ephors, a government of thirty citizens was put in place; Theramenes, an able man in both elocution and understanding,[14] and the high-flying but violent Critias (Plato's uncle) were their spokesmen. Instead of drawing up a new constitution, the Thirty seized absolute power with barely a word of protest from Lysander. At the Acropolis, a Spartan garrison was stationed under a harmost,[15] and the reign of the Thirty soon turned out to be one of terror; all troublesome elements were cleared away with the help of informants. No fewer than 1,500 Athenian citizens were executed, and many others – among them Thrasybulus[16] – survived only by fleeing. Thebes, Argos, Megara and other places granted them asylum. Ultimately, the terror of the Thirty came to an end.'[17]

In *Hellenica*, Xenophon describes the events as follows:[18] 'The Thirty had been chosen almost as soon the Long Walls and the fortifications around Piraeus had been razed. [...] Their task of renewing the old laws was never fulfilled. [...] Instead, they began punishing those who had proven themselves during the time of democracy to be opponents of the aristocracy. The courts set up specially to judge these people took drastic measures. In many cases, the sentence was death. Those who were not affected by them accepted these events without objection. In order to ensure their arbitrary measures could be enforced successfully, they forced Lysander to move a Spartan garrison to Athens. These men answered to the harmost Callibios, a man so corrupted by the Thirty, he approved of everything they did. Thus, they had Spartan soldiers at their disposal for all their undertakings. Gradually, they ceased confining themselves to pursuing solely the criminal element. Rather, they arrested whomsoever they thought might one day be a danger to them.'

Plato's Uncle

Critias, Plato's uncle, played a leading role in this drive: he had many of the people responsible for his exile by the demos – having been found to be an ally of Alcibiades shortly before the end of the war by the democratic warmonger Cleobulus and forced to emigrate to Thessaly – killed. Cleobulus was, even during the Spartan blockade, fanatically opposed to an agreement with Sparta.

Critias decisively rejected democracy in Athens and was a great friend to the Spartans. His beliefs were influenced by the Sophists and Socrates. With the stationing of 700 Spartan soldiers at the Acropolis, he went after the democrats with bloody terror. He eliminated his moderate rival Theramenes.[19]

Soon thereafter (in 403 BC), he fell in battle against Athens' democratic liberators, led by Thrasybulus[20] – Critias had realised the sophistic doctrine of 'might makes right' in the most brutal manner. One might think that his atrocities alone would be enough to prove the correctness of this doctrine.

If one were to allege that Critias, the radical opponent of democracy, had been a student of Socrates, this would not be without consequences. It was quite natural that Socrates should share some responsibility for Critias' crimes,[21] or be accused of 'guilt by association'.

Critias was also a prominent poet and writer.[22] Among other things, he wrote a satyr play with the title *Sisyphus*, in which he portrayed fear of the gods as an invention used to influence human behaviour. Law and justice are only suitable for ensuring an external order. To control 'secret transgressions', however, a clever mind invented religion. An omniscient deity might even look into human minds. The fear of the gods would, then, discourage them from evil acts. It is not to be dismissed out of hand that Critias himself used faith in the gods as an instrument of power.

Even Xenophon later made use of religious phenomena to influence people, for example by interpreting dreams as messages from the gods, and using them to support his intentions. A dream was instrumental, for example, in inspiring the Greek mercenaries not to give up after Cyrus' failed coup against the Persian king, and their hazardous retreat to the Black Sea.

Theramenes

The political programme of this Athenian politician was the establishment of a moderate oligarchy, but he also knew he had to come to an agreement with the democrats. This was presented to him as a betrayal of his oligarchic cause. Theramenes, however, was – in the eyes of Thucydides[23] and Xenophon[24] – only trying to bring about a balance between oligarchy and democracy: 'I have always fought against those who believe there can only be a good democracy if the slaves and the poor who would sell out the polis for a single drachma share in the government. I will, however, also oppose those who do not think that a good oligarchy can be established without the polis being ruled by a few.'[25] The middle ground that Theramenes represented was the requirement that those entitled to power be able to adequately arm themselves from their own resources in order to serve the polis.[26] Thus, only those who possessed a sufficient economic base would be able to vote.

Xenophon[27] lets Critias underline the political unreliability of Theramenes, making reference to his nickname for Theramenes, 'buskin,[28] a boot which fits either foot, which was supposed to illustrate the supposed fickleness of the politician: one moment Theramenes sympathised with the oligarchic party, the next, the democrats.

On the other hand, Aristotle[29] viewed Theramenes in a very positive light – perhaps under the influence of the philosophical serenity with which he drank the hemlock. Theramenes has a place – along with Nicias and Thucydides, son of Melesias, who distinguished himself in the fifth century BC as a leader of the oligarchical party and as an opponent of Pericles – among the greatest politicians of his time. Aristotle does not, however, conceal the fact that judgement of Theramenes was not universally positive – his country experienced serious unrest during his time. But those who look more closely must admit that Theramenes in no way destroyed all forms of government, and in fact encouraged a great many, so long as they had a legal basis. He was able to drive policy in all systems, which is, indeed, the duty of a good citizen. It was only illegal forms of government that he would not tolerate. This manifested itself in his deadly conflict with Critias.[30]

Theramenes was, incidentally, also a disciple of Socrates and the sophist Prodicus, and Thucydides attested to his political talent and great rhetorical skills.[31]

Since Theramenes was on friendly terms with Critias, he tried to talk him out of his criminal actions. It was unacceptable – according to Theramenes – to simply murder people because they had previously been regarded by the people as wanting to bring harm to aristocrats without ever actually having done anything. Critias, however, could not to be dissuaded. He justified his murders by citing the pressure on him to maintain power.

Theramenes suggested that the power base of the Thirty was too weak to keep the masses in check. Subsequently, Critias and the rest of the clique of tyrants drew up a list of 3,000 citizens who would share in the government. Apart from these 3,000 men, the entire population was disarmed with the help of the Lacedaemonians.

Shortly thereafter came the indiscriminate killing of numerous citizens – partly out of hostility, partly because for their wealth. To pay their Spartan friends, the Thirty demanded that each of the 3,000 citizens arrest a metic, kill him, and seize his assets.[32] Theramenes alone refused. It was unacceptable to Theramenes that those who considered themselves aristocrats could commit crimes more reprehensible than the actions of the professional informants, the notorious sycophants. They at least did not kill their victims. 'But shall we,' said Theramenes 'put people who are guilty of no wrong-doing to death, solely to take their money? Is that not a far greater crime than the actions of the sycophants?'[33]

This hit home. The Thirty decided to eliminate Theramenes. They slandered him as a public enemy, claiming he wanted to destroy the new political order of the oligarchs.

A council was then convened to decide the fate of Theramenes. To ensure their goal would prevail – if necessary with violence – the Thirty ordered several young men who were known to be particularly reliable, courageous and daring to arm themselves and be seen to be present in the council chambers.

One of these 'reliable, courageous and daring' young men was Xenophon of Athens.[34] He was thus able to listen to the speeches of the two opponents, quickly note down their key messages, and later record them in his Greek history.[35]

When Theramenes appeared, Critias began his speech to the Athenian councillors by pointing out that it was normal for many people to die during a political upheaval.[36] He made no secret about removing the enemies of the oligarchy, and his desire to be particularly harsh on opponents in his own ranks. This also included Theramenes – for he had brought the oligarchs into disrepute like nothing else. He objected whenever it came down to killing a former leader of the people. He was a dangerous traitor to the oligarchic cause, and to the interests of their Spartan liberators. He deserved death.

Theramenes defended himself with aplomb, and it was expected that the city council would absolve him of all guilt. The proceedings were broken off, but Critias wanted to prevent Theramenes' acquittal. After a brief discussion with the other oligarchs, Critias ordered the young men to draw their weapons for everyone to see. He then addressed the council anew: 'The men standing here will not accept the release of a man who undoubtedly wants to destroy the oligarchy.'

He demanded the death penalty. The councillors were so intimidated, they could not refuse. Theramenes was arrested at once and immediately forced to drink hemlock.

After his death, the Thirty had no further concerns about extending their arbitrary measures. Countless Athenians fled Athens as a result. Arbitrary arrests were common. The oligarchs had their eyes on the assets and land of rich citizens. The slightest suspicion was enough for the Thirty to have the owner openly murdered. Neither democrats nor supporters of the aristocracy were spared. Even staunch opponents of democracy, who had been sentenced to exile by a democratic court years earlier and were allowed to return after the end of the war, fell victim to the tyrants.

Xenophon of Athens

We can assume that Xenophon was born in Athens between 430 and 425, and did not die before 355 BC. Shortly before the expulsion of the Thirty Tyrants, he was invited by his friend Proxenus to come to Sardis. Proxenus wanted to introduce him to Cyrus, the younger brother of the Great King. 'To be allowed access to the circle of friends of such an extraordinary personality must have been a very attractive idea for a philosophically educated and open-minded man such as Xenophon. There is, of course, a second motive to consider: Xenophon had apparently served in the Athenian cavalry under the Thirty in the final years of the Peloponnesian war – their sympathisers had a hard time in Athens after the restoration of democracy in Athens in

403. It is possible that he wanted to disappear for a while, and receiving the letter from Proxenus was simply a good opportunity to do so.'[37]

So Xenophon joined the campaign of the Persian prince Cyrus against his brother, the Great King of Persia. The undertaking failed in September 401 BC with the death of Cyrus at the Battle of Cunaxa, about 90km north-east of Babylon. The Ten Thousand Greek mercenaries, however, remained undefeated and unwilling to submit to the Persian king.

After the assassination of the Greek generals by the Persian satrap Tissaphernes, Xenophon was, surprisingly, chosen as strategist to succeed the dead Proxenus.[38] He led the army to the coast of the Black Sea, and in Pergamus, in the spring of 399 BC, he put the army under the control of the Spartan general Thibron.

In the mid-390s BC, Xenophon joined the Spartan king Agesilaus, who undertook several military campaigns against Tissaphernes in Asia Minor. In the company of the king, he returned to Greece in 394 BC, and took the side of the Spartans at the Battle of Coronea in Boeotia,[39] in which the Spartans, under Agesilaus, effortlessly defeated the army of Boeotians, Athenians, Corinthians, and others.

Xenophon's participation in this battle, on the side of the Spartans, is likely what led to his banishment in the year 394 BC at the request of the Athenian archon Eubulus.[40] Between 399 and 387 BC, Xenophon married Philesia[41] and his sons Gryllus and Diodorus were born. At the beginning of the 380s BC, the Spartans granted him a piece of land and a house in Skillus in the north-west Peloponnese,[42] to reward him for his service to Sparta.

After the Spartans were defeated in the Battle of Leuctra in 371 BC, Xenophon and his family had to leave Skillus. His final residence was probably in Corinth.[43] In the course of the rapprochement between Athens and Sparta, his banishment was repealed in 368 or 367 BC – at the request of the same ruler who had originally demanded he be banished.[44] Xenophon reclaimed his wealth in Attica. His sons, Gryllus and Diodorus, who had been educated in Sparta, served in the Athenian cavalry. Gryllus was slain in cavalry engagement just before the Battle of Mantinea in 362 BC, in which the legendary Theban general Epaminondas defeated a combined army of Athenians and Spartans.

It can be assumed that Xenophon died sometime after 355 BC at around the age of 70.[45]

Conjecture about Thucydides

There were reports of the death of Thucydides circulating even in ancient times. It is all too easy to trace the abrupt end of his historical work on the Peloponnesian war to an act of violence.

'That Thucydides died a "violent death", as claimed by the learned Didymus, was certainly the unanimous belief in ancient times. According to Didymus, Thucydides was killed in Athens during the era of the Thirty; according to Plutarch, he was murdered on his estate in Skapte Hyle near the gold mines of Pangaion. His grave was discovered by an archaeologist, Polemon of Ilios, 200 years later in Athens amongst the graves of the family of Cimon. That was when the concern over the nature, place, and circumstances of the death of Thucydides began.'[46]

Xenophon, who continued the work of Thucydides practically at the point where Thucydides had stopped writing, had been banished from Athens for decades without ever having said a single word of clarification on the matter.

'It is impossible to do anything more than speculate about the circumstances of Thucydides' death. The ancient sources provide so many different versions of his death that the obvious suspicion is that antiquity has no more reliable information than we do. Marcellinus, who discussed the matter in the most detail (31–33) cited witnesses who claimed to have knowledge of a death in Thrace. At the same time, he was aware of legends that Thucydides had supposedly died in Italy. Other stories say he met his end in a shipwreck. Pausanias (1.23.8) claims that Thucydides was murdered as he was returning to Athens from exile. He says as little about the (alleged) murder as Plutarch, who is also aware of the version of a violent death, but reproduces it differently (Cimon 4): Thucydides died in Thrace, in the town of Skapte Hyle, murdered, and his remains were brought to Attica, where his monument is shown amongst the graves of Cimon's family, besides Elpinice, Cimon's sister. How the conclusion that Thucydides was murdered was reached can no longer be reconstructed, and can, moreover, not be excluded. After all, the political situation in Athens in the post-war period was unstable enough to be dangerous to a critical spirit such as Thucydides.'[47]

But who stood to gain from killing the historian? The Thirty, with the intention of taking his assets, or those who had been embarrassed by him? Athenian patriots who saw him as a Spartan sympathiser? He himself points out in the second preface of his historical work (5.26) that he had to live in exile for twenty years after his military failure in Amphipolis.[48] He naturally had contact with the Peloponnesians during this time, who could provide him with information for his historical work.

Another motive for his violent elimination could have been his negative portrayal of the radical democrat Cleon.[49] Thucydides had after all named him the 'most violent man' in Athens. The fact that the historian also spoke confidently and with a certain arrogance of his scientific achievements could have provoked the envious and the resentful to an act of violence. He once, for example, justified one of his analyses with the words '… because I know it, and I have a more specific knowledge of events than any other.'[50]

The possibility that Thucydides brought events to light with his very thorough research[51] that would impact heavily on those concerned must also be taken seriously – those involved would have wanted to stop the completion of Thucydides' work by any means possible.[52]

Xenophon Recalls: In the Service of The Thirty

My martial appearance in that memorable council meeting to determine the fate of Theramenes, led to serious allegations later. Yes – I was among those young men who were to intimidate the council on the order of Critias with their presence. I admit that. But the idea that I was otherwise involved of the machinations of the Thirty? Never. I have not participated in any of the many arrests, nor did I have anything to do with the death of Thucydides – of course I didn't. To assert otherwise is absurd.[53] Quite the opposite, in fact – I did everything in my power to protect him from the Thirty.

I don't deny that I took part in the battles against Thrasybulus as a cavalryman. I recorded in detail everything I saw in my Hellenica,[54] and revealed therein that I respected Thrasybulus, even though I stood against him.

When, after the disastrous defeat of the Athenian forces, the Thirty took power, I thought myself lucky, as the cavalry in which I had served as a very young man was immediately put under the command of the Thirty after the surrender. So did the Spartans decree, attempting to restore public order by any means. We were happy that the Spartans hadn't simply dismissed us. So we were allowed to continue our service, but now we were safe. I didn't care from whom my orders came – that I admit.

We were given the barracks in which the hippo-toxotai – the mounted archers – had been housed until the end of the war, which were not in use. The first generation of hippo-toxotai – we called them the grandfathers – had been 'bought' right after the end of the Persian war in Scythia. Eventually, thetes – the unpropertied, but free Athenian citizens – were added to the troop. The

City made weapons and horses available to these people. They had the task of ensuring peace and order in Athens and in Attica, especially in public assemblies, theatre performances and court proceedings. They wore a tall, pointed hat, a bow, an animal-skin quiver on their left side, attached to a belt, a short sword – sometimes an axe as well – and long pantaloons, reaching to the ankles. Most referred to them after these 'pantaloons', which were particularly striking in Athens, but very practical. They were not soldiers, but police. During the war, however, they were used as soldiers. Because they lacked proper combat training, they were hopelessly inferior to the Spartan hoplites, and suffered heavy losses. After the peace agreement, the remaining 'pantaloons' – there were scarcely 400 of the original 1,000 men remaining – were incorporated into our cavalry.

I was very glad, at the time, to be allowed to stay in Athens, although I could have had a peaceful life on our estate near the city. But who wouldn't have wanted to live in Athens?

Although we were clearly different from our new comrades, the 'pantaloons', or, officially, 'anaxyrides' – not only in appearance, but also in our backgrounds and education as mounted ephebes – we got along with them extremely well. There were no significant difficulties. Quite the opposite – the anaxyrides were always a particular attraction at our military exercises and daily parades. They shone with their daring acrobatics and always had plenty of enthusiastic spectators. It was amazing how well they mastered their horses.

Our ten squadrons – each Attican Phyle contributed a squadron – demonstrated their skills with utmost order and discipline. Unlike the hoplites, we had no lustrous bronze greaves, but rather high leather boots so as not to injure our horses' flanks. We wore hoplite armour and a shield only during parades. A sword and two spears were among our permanent equipment.

I will not deny that we felt superior to the rank and file hoplites. We weren't, of course. But such feelings were easy to explain when you looked down from your horses on the soldiers on foot. But did our great comic playwright Aristophanes, in his play The Knights, with which in the very year of my birth[55] he won first prize at the Lenaia festival,[56] really have the right to call us arrogant aristocrats? Perhaps he was influenced by the artful depiction of the ephebes of the cavalry by Pheidias, our great sculptor?

The allegations levelled against me as a result of my presence in that fateful council made me realise for the first time that I had been made the henchman of a criminal regime. Very soon, I had the opportunity to prove that I was not merely the tool of the Thirty – one evening, I was in a building in which the Thirty had retired for deliberation, and I witnessed a conversation. What I heard troubled me greatly: 'He must be silenced – he knows too much', exclaimed an agitated voice from behind the tightly closed door. I understood the words perfectly. It seemed as though I was supposed to listen to them.

'Why did we even consider bringing him back to Athens?' demanded one of the Thirty, who had been meeting regularly for months, each time in a different location. No one was supposed to know what they were discussing – especially not 'our Spartan friends' in the Acropolis who sought to establish order in Athens after the war, and would support the Thirty by any means to achieve this aim. The government in Sparta had assigned the supreme command to highly deserving Admiral Lysander[57] in Athens to reward him for his successful surrender negotiations. The war-hero had sunk twenty Athenian ships at Notion near Ephesus in winter of the twenty-fourth year of the war. I secretly admired him for that – even more for the annihilation of the Athenian fleet on the beaches of Aigospotamoi.[58]

'He's lived off his Thracian gold for twenty years,' I heard another voice say after a while.

'Yes... it certainly hasn't gone badly for him in Skapte Hyle,' someone laughed.

'We will send for him tomorrow, at sunrise,' explained Critias in a firm voice that would permit no contradiction. 'Lysimachus already has the orders. He will send some of his most trusted men to Thucydides' home. They will ask him to accompany them, but they will not resort to violence. Then the thing will be done in silence.

Now, suddenly, I knew why we had to be present outside the courtroom. In that moment, the door opened. Critias was the first to emerge, the others huddled behind him. They spoke animatedly with each other, but I couldn't make out a word.

I had previously only seen Critias once or twice before from a distance, and didn't know much about him beyond his speech to the council against Theramenes.

In private, people whispered that he was a close friend – as Alcibiades had been – of Socrates, but that he was the greediest, most violent, most blood-thirsty of all the oligarchs. Quite the opposite of Alcibiades, then, the most extravagant, boisterous and unpredictable politician,[59] who was completely indifferent as to who paid him, and who therefore regularly switched sides.

Alcibiades

Alcibiades, born in 450 BC, was related to Pericles. Socrates had saved his life in the Battle of Potidaea (432 BC). Eight years later, he is said to have saved Socrates from certain death at Delion. He played a leading role in all campaigns in the Peloponnesian war. Among other things, he led the so-called Sicilian expedition which ended so catastrophically for the Athenians. He changed sides many times, before finally going to Persia – defecting to the satrap Pharnabazus – where he was killed in 404/403 BC on the order of the Spartan Lysander and the Thirty Tyrants.[60]

'But the essence and – in view of his possible pursuit of tyranny – the danger of his work... lay in the fact that in this man gifted with uncommon ability and bewitching grace, there was a personality that, true to the spirit of his radical Sophist teachings, had no qualms arrogantly defying custom and convention. As long as he could influence judges and the populous with the charm of his personality, he was irresistible. A man who was ultimately a law unto himself.'[61]

Thucydides saw Alcibiades' true driving force behind his immense ambition (5.43.2). His pride came with exaggerated egotism and self-obsession (6.12.2). His lifestyle was costly and excessive (6.15).[62] His intellectual superiority and military capability were fascinating (6.15.4). In a speech in which he campaigned for the Sicilian expedition of 415 BC, he clearly confessed to an aristocratic, anti-democratic attitude: 'It is in any case unfair that the principle of equality be suspended for someone who has great thoughts. Even for those at the very bottom, this principle does not apply. For as one is unnoticed when badly off, so too must we bear to be ignored by those who are doing well' (6.16.4).[63]

For Alcibiades, natural inequality was therefore incontrovertible fact. Politically, this was the main argument of the aristocratic oligarchic party against the democratic pursuit of 'equality'. It remains doubtful, however, whether Alcibiades ever actually felt connected to a certain party. According to everything that is known of him, he likely had his own interests in mind – interests he would seek to ruthlessly enforce.[64]

Socrates

After the departure of the Thirty, Socrates (469 BC–399 BC) was sentenced by an Athenian court to death by hemlock. The official reason for the death sentence was based on the charge that Socrates had forsaken the gods of the state religion and led the youth astray by introducing foreign gods.[65] Exactly what was meant by these charges could not be understood even by Socrates' contemporaries. For Xenophon, the accusations against Socrates were incomprehensible.[66]

Socrates' friends repeatedly emphasized his obedience to the law, his moral fortitude and his credibility. Plato[67] has him explain: 'I have never held any other office in the state, but I was once a senator ... when you wished to judge collectively the ten generals who failed to rescue the shipwrecked after the naval Battle of Arginusae [a small group of islands between Lesbos and the coast of Asia Minor] – this was illegal, as you later accepted. At the time, I was the only senator who objected, and urged you not to do anything contrary to the laws. That is why I voted against the proceedings. And although your spokesman intended to officially denounce and immediately arrest me, as you so loudly demanded, I believed myself to be on the side of justice, and that I had to take the risk, rather than obey you out of fear of imprisonment or death. Your wishes were unjust. This was when democracy still existed.' (406 BC)

Even Xenophon notes in *Hellenica*[68] that Socrates was the only one who objected to committing an illegal act, and Plato has Socrates say:[69] 'After the oligarchy was established, the Thirty sent for me and four others to come to the rotunda. They ordered us to bring Leon, the Salaminian from Salamis, to put him to death, as they ordered many others, because the wanted to implicate as many in their crimes as they could. I, however, showed again – not only in words but with actions – that my own death was unimportant to me, if that not be too rude a statement, but that it was more important to me not to do anything unjust or unholy. For the power of the Thirty could not – even if they had not been so violent – compel me to do something unjust but when we left the rotunda, the other four went to Salamis and arrested Leon, and I simply went home. Perhaps I would have been put to death for it, had the oligarchy not shortly thereafter been put down.'

But Socrates nevertheless seems still to have been associated with the hated regime – likely due to his relationship with Critias. Even Plato, his most famous student, was anything but a friend of Athenian democracy. It is also not forgotten that Xenophon, whose association with Socrates was no secret, had served the terror regime in his youth, and represented Spartan interests far from Athens. The fact that Socrates was hardly a 'resistance fighter' amongst the Thirty, and remained unmolested in Athens rather than emigrating like so many others, must also have compromised the philosopher.[70] Socrates' alleged atheism should not be underestimated. The philosopher never lost the image of a 'godless' sophist. It cannot be overlooked that in those dramatic times of uncertainty after the catastrophe of the war, a violation of religious sensibilities – even a putative violation – could have deadly consequences.

It should also be questioned whether the 'amnesty' urged by Thrasybulus – which benefited the followers of the Thirty after the re-establishment of democracy – was really universally accepted. It is quite conceivable[71] that an unsatisfied desire for revenge for crimes committed by the oligarchy influenced the negotiations against Socrates. It can be concluded, then, that Socrates may have been sentenced as a representative for the unpunished oligarchic 'perpetrators'. If a fair trial of the oligarchic perpetrators had taken place, Socrates might never have been summoned to appear before the court.

The Comedy Writer

If Critias had really killed 1,500 influential democrats,[72] then one could blame his teacher Socrates for laying the intellectual groundwork for these crimes. Despite the lack of evidence for Socrates' complicity in the murders committed by the Thirty, this assumption was enough for him to be called before the court. This was added to by the fact that Socrates was discriminated against and ridiculed at every conceivable turn by politically influential comedy writers – in particular by Aristophanes, in his play *The Clouds* – as a 'sophist'.[73]

The comedy, in which Socrates was the protagonist, took its name from the Chorus of the Clouds, the gods of the modern age – that is, from the thoughts, ideas, concepts and clever tricks of the dialectical philosophy and sophist rhetoric. The simple peasant Strepsiades faces financial ruin. He can no longer maintain the life his demanding wife and spoiled son want to lead, but he sees a way out: the young Pheidippides, Strepsiades' son, will attend Socrates' school, 'the Thoughtery'. There, he will learn the art of turning inferior arguments into winning arguments at court under Chaerephon and Socrates. The boy refuses, so Strepsiades decides to learn with Socrates himself instead. He is taken on as a student, but is hardly capable of understanding the basics of higher education, and so his son must take his place at the school anyway. In a debate, 'Superior Argument' and 'Inferior Argument' offer to be his teacher. Pheidippides gives his preference to 'Inferior Argument', and begins to learn how his father can escape the attentions of the meddling creditors. But then there is an argument between father and son: Pheidippides physically beats his own father. He tells his father that this treatment is entirely fair, as he once learned from his father.

Strepsiades cannot accept what has been taught to his son, and he sets Socrates' Thoughtery on fire.

This comedy was born out of the poet's struggle with the alleged 'corrupting, new-fangled educational ideals that, due to the work of sophist enlightenment, were becoming ever more popular in Athens'.[74] Plato asserts in *Apology* that Aristophanes' Socrates character was one of the triggers for the philosopher's trial. There is, however, no evidence that Aristophanes deliberately sought to get Socrates into trouble in 423 BC.

Thucydides in Danger?

> This had not occurred to me when I confronted Critias. All I knew was that the talk about him and Alcibiades could have a fatal effect on the fate of the respected teacher.
>
> I had no such dark thoughts when he turned to me. 'Ah, who do we have here? Xenophon, son of noble Gryllus, of the deme Erchia?' exclaimed Critias with feigned warmth. I was surprised that he would address me by name – and with such amicability! But his surprise was faked – he knew full well that I would be waiting here with my friends Leontychus and Crinippus for orders from our Hipparchus Lysimachus. Of course, it was not clear to us why. We were initially mandated only to protect the meeting room from unwanted visitors, and to stand by for further duties. So far, nothing out of the ordinary had happened, so we could have returned to our quarters.
>
> But then I heard the apparent danger to Thucydides and his planned arrest. What did that mean? Would we be required for that, of all things? That was – at least for now – not the case. If we really were to arrest him the next morning, then we would only receive our orders shortly beforehand – 'in order to ensure confidentiality', they said. But then why had Critias let us know what was going to happen tomorrow? Had he spoken so loudly about this issue so we would hear? What did Critias want? Should we warn Thucydides of his impending arrest? Or should we just let him know the quickest way back to Thrace? Even that would betray to him that he was a danger. How could you simply turn a man like that loose? Perhaps this was – as I suspected – simply the language regime of Critias' oligarchic colleagues. In reality, his intention was not to invoke the dangerous nature of the historian, but simply to indicate the danger he was in. Then Critias would conspire with me and my comrades against the majority of the Thirty. An absurd idea!
>
> I later learned that there were numerous boxes and baskets filled with papers, documents, letters and books in Thucydides' home. It was material for his history book, which he had not yet completed despite starting the moment the

Great War had begun, and working on it for the twenty years he had unwillingly been away from Athens. Immediately after the war, he was about to complete it.

At the time, I didn't understand how the writer could be as 'dangerous' as Critias had so loudly claimed. Nor could I imagine that he was the kind of man to flee, if he were really so dangerous to the regime of the Thirty. I had no explanation for it, and could only speculate. Critias and Thucydides were about the same age – almost sixty. This was not insignificant for a poet. He had studied with the sophists. His closeness to Socrates was no secret. He was also acquainted with prominent sophists – among them, Protagoras of Abdera, who was also a friend of Pericles. There was no doubt that he held Socrates in high regard. It was quite possible that the two were linked in far more than simply their age and aristocratic origin. Could this uncomfortable truth have been discovered by the people around Critias?

If it were true that the Thirty had killed almost as many Athenians in the last eight months alone as the Peloponnesians had in the last ten years of the war, then it would be very dangerous to know more about it than the general public.

The Sophists

The Sophists, the teachers of wisdom, were among the first to respond productively to the political and social signs of disintegration after the devastating, but finally successful Persian wars (490–479 BC), and to expose the dubious nature of the order that remained. They started an education system, consisting mainly of criticising the ruling theology and questioning the traditional value system. They raised awareness that one's chance to prevail in an unstable world was essentially based on the mastery of language – with the help of Language, one would be able to justify one's purpose, or reject what one did not want.

The conviction that a man could be assertive and successful through the purposeful use of language allowed the rhetoric and science of using language to achieve political and personal objectives to become an essential factor in the education of the youth. Socrates, however, saw the potential for language to be abused, and warned that the rhetoric must be wielded not only with serious knowledge, but also with a sense of responsibility.

An attribute common to all sophists was their clear commitment to anthropocentrism, in that they declared – with the so-called Homo Mensura statement – that Man was the focus of all that happened in the world: 'Man is the measure of all things'.[75]

'Things' in the Homo Mensura statement referred to the diversity of the world in relation to the people who live in it. 'Thus, because man confronts, perceives, creates, is able to use more precisely the things in the world, he reshapes them as his own, i.e., he makes them into a world that belongs to him. He becomes the yardstick by which they are measured. […]This anthropogenic world view conceptualises man as a creature that re-coins the world available to it as a 'world' it can avail itself of. […]With the idea of use as a category that defines the relationship of man to the things in the world and defines the status of man as the yardstick by which his world is measured, Protagoras introduced a central concept to anthropocentrism which was later shaped and enriched, and passed on, by Aristotle, Xenophon, the Stoics in particular, and early Christianity.'[76]

Memories of the Parthenon Frieze

My involvement in the machinations of the Thirty began in my childhood, when no one would have guessed this regime would one day take hold.

I can still clearly remember my father explaining the Parthenon frieze on the acropolis. I was just ten years old.[77] The end of the inter-war period was already on the horizon. We rode to Athens.

'Before war breaks out again…' my father said. 'The truce has lasted six years and ten months. We should use our time before it ends.'

In Athens, we found accommodation for the horses with a fellow trader in a spacious barn. My father made sure they had dry straw and enough hay to eat. 'The horses always come first,' he used to say. 'First the animals, then man!' I never forgot that. The owner of the stall had obviously made preparations.

We went then to a stonemason called Kresilas. He was one of the artists who had created the decoration of the Parthenon under the guidance of Pheidias. My father obviously knew the old man. After a short welcome, he handed us each a leather apron and a felt cap. I wondered to myself, why? I felt quite uneasy. Both the hat and the apron were far too large for me. But my father simply said: 'You have to wear it now, or we can't go into the temple. We have to take the box of chisels and hammers, too.'

The stonemason led us to a group of men who were loading a cart with tools and equipment. We were welcomed warmly and asked to put our stuff on the cart. Slowly, I realised we were to join up with the workers. But why? 'What are we doing here?' I asked my father quietly.

'Just wait! You'll find out soon,' answered my father.

I kept quiet. The cart set off. We followed it on foot alongside the workers. Kresilas called out to us:

'Good luck! Come back safe – don't lose a finger, or fall from the scaffold!'

After a few steps I saw my father smile: 'We're sculptors now. We're going to help these people in their work.' Now I realised we needed these disguises to even enter the interior of the Parthenon.

'The last earthquake left its mark on the acropolis,' said one of the workers to me, when I looked at him questioningly. 'Good that you want to help out, kid,' he added jokingly.

'Happy to,' I replied, somewhat surprised, 'If I really can help.'

'Well, we'll see.'

Finally, the cart stopped. We had to climb a ridiculous number of steps to reach the top. Everyone carried their own tools. Finally, we reached the Temple of the Virgin, the house Pericles had built for the goddess Athena a few years before the outbreak of the Great War. I was out of breath and very excited.

Inside the temple, below the roof beams, practically four foot high, the frieze covered all four wars. 'It's almost a full stadion long,' said my father as I gazed upwards in astonishment. Under the frieze, a scaffold was erected on one side. It was easily thirty feet high, and helped the workers to reach the places that were being repaired. That's what they were doing now, with great zeal. They were largely unconcerned with me and my father. Nobody expected to use our hammer and chisel on the frieze, or to bring plaster and cement up. 'You see the procession here, starting at the Eleusis gate on Sacred way, moving through the city to the acropolis? There are the priests, the maids of honour, the water-bearers, or hydrophores, the leader of the sacrificial animals and musicians'. Gryllus described the frieze to me. I listened, speechless, but attentive.

We went a little further. My father pointed upwards again:

'...and here are the mounted ephebes that accompany the procession – you can see almost 400 people and 200 animals here!' I wanted to count them, but we quickly moved on.

'Imagine if everything up there was really moving, if the horse stomped and snorted and whinnied! Isn't it incredible?' Gryllus exclaimed, excited. I silently agreed with him. I stared, fascinated, at a rider with his left hand stretched out over his head, the collection of his horse almost exaggerated. You could see and feel how powerfully and obediently it would gallop. A magnificent image!

'You can see how important it is to train your horse, to ensure it readily provides its strength in the service of its rider. Only when you achieve this objective can horse and rider participate in the procession to honour the goddess.'

'I want to learn how,' I interjected.

'Yes, you ought to know that this can only be achieved with much effort and hard work… but you will definitely make it if you keep this up!' My father's words made me happy. He always encouraged me to overcome difficulties, and he never let me down when I needed his help. If I ever thanked him, he would only ever whisper:

'Your grandfather was the same with me.'

But I was never permitted to ride in the panathenaic procession. Once I began my service as an ephebe, the long war against Sparta was lost, and in the confusion of the immediate post-war period, there were no processions. Instead, we ephebes became the mounted bodyguards of the Thirty. To this day I do not know whether my father seriously had my honourable participation in the procession in mind when he took me to the Parthenon. I never doubted that it was a worthy goal to strive for.

When we went back down the steps of the Parthenon, still wearing our sculptor disguises, I was determined to become one of those people in the frieze. The gods, however, intended otherwise, and the circumstances of time were not favourable. At the time, I had no idea.

I never saw the frieze again. I read the great Epitaphios of Pericles in the historical works of Thucydides[78] many years later, and was vividly reminded of the image of those figures once again.

Thucydides' Epitaphios

In the winter of 431/430 BC, a public funeral was held for the first of those killed in the Peloponnesian War. For this reason, Pericles, son of Xanthippus, was chosen to give the epitaphios. He found it hard to find the right balance of truth in his words. Before addressing the deeds of the fallen, he wanted to explain what the majority of the Athenian populace relied on, and with what kind of lifestyle, political constitution, temperamental prerequisites and attitude towards life the Athenians had achieved their success.

The Athenian constitution was democratic, because it was not controlled by a few men, but by the majority. Every individual was the same in the eyes of the law. This isonomy was the most important part of Athenian democracy. Public appreciation arose not from membership to a certain class, but from a person's accomplishments. No one was prevented from contributing to society solely due to a lack of resources or because of humble origins. All citizens were free to work for the common good, and were considerate of each other in daily life.

'Unlike our enemies, we Athenians rely less on external preparation and deceit than on our own courage in action. While the Spartans are familiar with rigorous exercises in bravery from their childhood education, we live without coercion and restriction, yet still dare to take on the same risks as they. […] But if we prefer to place ourselves in danger with easy, unburdened meaning, rather than with painstaking effort, and rely less on legally prescribed courage than on natural bravery, then we have the advantage, because we do not labour under then expectation of a coming disaster, but face it with no less determination than those who do.'[79]

The ephebes in the Parthenon frieze express this perfectly. They dash in, apparently at random, but sparkling with joy and confidence, the awesome power of their horses firmly under their control – those young men, who with the expressions on their faces, with the slightest tilt of their heads, make you feel as though they were riding under the eyes of the gods.[80]

Pericles continued his speech with the following words (2.40): 'We live in beauty without excess, and we cultivate knowledge without sacrificing vigour. We use material resources where necessary, and not for show. Admitting to poverty is a disgrace for no man, but to do nothing about it is shameful. We can reconcile private and public interests – even if we toil with other matters, we do not neglect our public duties. […]We either make political decisions ourselves, or we think clearly about them. We do not believe that discussion is detrimental to action, but rather that far more damage is done if one acts without thought…'

The Order

Lost in thought, I looked again into the stable. Everything was quiet; only the chewing of the horses to be heard. Then I lay down to sleep. Lysimachus woke us early in the morning:

'You. With me!' He pointed at me, Leontychus and Crinippus. 'I have new orders for you.'

A short while later we stood before him as he described our mission – a mission we had known was coming for a long time.

'But no violence! Critias commands it. I'm relying on you.'

We set off on foot so as not to attract attention. It was still dark in the streets of Athens.

Thucydides' home was not easy to find, being no different from any other Athenian house. These consist of a large main room, the oikos, with other, smaller rooms leading off it. These served as bedrooms, kitchens and storage rooms. That the Athenians place so little value on designing cosy town houses can be explained by their way of life: they spend most of their time on the streets. They go to their jobs as craftsmen, then they go to the market, visit the courtrooms, theatres, public squares, the gymnasia. Thucydides, however, had as far as I could see transformed his oikos into a study – he had set up an armchair, two folding stools and a small table. The chest containing his papers and books

needed for his work was not among the furnishings. It had been placed in a
storage space behind or under the kitchen. When he needed something, he would
disappear, returning with the required papers and scrolls.

Behind an Athenian house, you can usually find a small garden, which you
could enter or leave through a narrow door in the back wall. I didn't know at this
point that there was a small cellar under the kitchen in Thucydides' house where
you could keep food cool. Nor was I aware that this vault was accessible through
a trapdoor in the kitchen floor via a ladder, which stood reasonably safely on the
hard-packed cellar floor.

We reached the high outer-wall from the street. A low gate led into a small,
partly covered atrium. We agreed that I would enter alone to request as kindly as
possible that Thucydides come with us. But what if he refused?

I wasn't sure, but I had an adventurous plan, of which I told my two
companions nothing: I intended to persuade the writer to leave Athens as soon as
possible. That was against my orders, admittedly, but I wanted to make amends.
I would simply tell Lysimachus that we hadn't found the man – it would appear
that he had already fled in the night.

Thucydides: Biography and Historical Work

Thucydides, born around 460 BC (4.104) was presumably still living by
the end of the war. His history book, the unfinished monograph on the
Peloponnesian war (431–404 BC) in eight books offers the most reliable
information about his life. The account breaks off after the events of the
autumn of 411 BC. Obviously, the son of Olorus had conducted thorough
historiographical preparation for his writing, and, before beginning his
work, undertaken methodological deliberations, which he included in the
so-called 'Archaeology' section – the core of the preface (1.2–21) – and
elaborated on in the 'Methods' chapter (1.22).

In the preface, Thucydides points out that he began his records at the
beginning of the war because he recognized the incredible magnitude of the
disaster from the start. In the so-called second preface (5.26), he states that
he had witnessed twenty-seven years of war.

As a member of an important Athenian noble family, the son of Olorus
was an active politician and military officer, but for his strategic failure
in northern Greece, he was exiled for twenty years from 424 BC. He gives
the reason for his exile in connection with his account of the capture of
Amphipolis by the Spartan Brasidas (4.104 f.).[81] Only after the lost war
(404 BC) was Thucydides allowed to return to Athens, but he lived well in

the meantime on the profits from his mine in Thrace. It is not clear, however, whether he actually spent the years of his exile in Thrace. In his writing (5.26), he mentions being in contact with two warring parties, which was helpful for his work.

The idea that the incomplete eighth book of his writing was composed by Thucydides' daughter or by Xenophon is mentioned by Marcellinus (43), but excluded. His reasoning, however, is more than questionable: 'Some claim the eighth book does not originate with Thucydides. Instead, some say it was written by his daughter, some see Xenophon as the writer. To this we reply: It is impossible that the book was written by his daughter, because it is not of the womanly nature to imitate such ability and artfulness as is evident in the other books. If this were however the case, then the woman would not have sought to remain hidden behind the work, and would not have written only this eighth book, but would have left many other books behind to demonstrate her ability. That the eighth book is not by Xenophon, however, is obvious from the style (of the eighth book), which differs from his plain and not elevated style.'

Thucydides' life was shaped by one event among many others described in his work: the great epidemic (2.47–54), which claimed innumerable lives in Athens in 430 BC. The historian himself was afflicted with the disease (2.45), which was commonly referred to as 'the plague', without being able to accurately diagnose the disease.

The account deals initially with the decade-long 'Archidamian War' (431 BC to 421 BC).[82] There are, however, indications in the first part of this work that it was written after 404 BC, and in the so-called 'second preface', the author reveals that he regards the entire war from 431 BC to 404 BC to be the single subject of his account, but has composed his work in two stages: the first, which concerns only the Archidamian War, and a second, which covers the entire war. The philological argument over whether or not Thucydides himself penned the work, however, leads only to the conclusion that by far the largest part of the text of the first books could have been written either before or after 421 BC, or soon after 404 BC.

Thucydides describes the historical events not only by a chronological account, but also by speeches constructed himself, but ostensibly spoken by the persons concerned. He divides events into seasonally defined sections, occasionally interrupted by digressions from the account. He characterizes the dialogues as his own creations (1.22.1). Taking into account the overall tenor of a real speech, he created new dialogues and monologues that closely approximate the intentions of the speakers and make the sequence of events easy to understand. These speeches prove to be an essential element of the composition of his work. The most famous examples are Pericles' epitaphios for the fallen (2.35–46), and a further speech during the time of the plague (2.47–54 and 59–64). In addition, Thucydides makes use of the form of speech 'agons', or contests. This allows, for example, Alcibiades and Nicias to have a verbal clash before the Sicilian expedition (6.9–23).

Dividing events by seasons enabled Thucydides to include all events over the course of a year in natural time-order, maximising accuracy in a time before a uniform calendar had been achieved. The tally of the war years also added to this.

Thucydides' most famous digression is the description of the so-called 'Pentecontaetia' – the period of approximately fifty years between the Persian king Xerxes withdrawing from Greece and the beginning of the Peloponnesian war (1.118.2). It consists of an account of many details from Greek history between 479 BC and 431 BC, purporting to be a summary of a comprehensive history of Greece.

There are no literary models for the topic of Thucydides' book. An examination of Herodotus' view of historiography is however evident: Thucydides' emphatically distances himself from the entertainment function present in works based on Herodotus' theory, instead using all the sources of information available to him pertaining to contemporary events, and makes use of the results of his detailed examination of these events. He placed particular importance on representing 'his' war as the greatest of all wars (1.21.2), and downplaying the significance of the Persian wars described by Herodotus, for the publication of Herodotus' historical work reawakened memories of a glorious defensive battle, threatening to relegate Thucydides' account to second place. Thus Thucydides had no other but to downplay the importance of the Persian wars.

Even the author's famous statement of intent to create an 'everlasting possession' with his work (1.22.4) must be seen against the background of his polemic against Herodotus: 'Only with difficulty have the facts been established, as the testimonies of the witnesses of the events were not often the same, but was defined in each individual's perspective by their sympathies or powers of recall. This sober and factual account of events will perhaps appear less appealing to the audience; if however there is anyone who intends to understand what actually occurred – and that something like this will, according to human nature, one day occur again – then it is enough for me that my remarks be considered useful. This account is compiled as an everlasting possession, and not as something for a moment's pleasure.'

The reader should, then, perceive the account as 'useful', and its 'usefulness' should continue to apply in the future, since according to 'human nature', a repetition of the events described is to be expected. The reader should therefore learn something for the future handling of similar events (cf. 2.48.3).

The fact that humanity does not change is the force that defines history for Thucydides. He defines it[83] as a constant pattern of behaviour. This is in contrast to Herodotus' 'theonomic' interpretation of history. The 'typical human' belief that 'might makes right' is a reason for war: competition between great powers for supremacy. Obviously, Thucydides wanted to prove with the example of the Peloponnesian war (again, unlike Herodotus) that historical cycles can be explained through the effectiveness of 'human' and not a 'higher' power. War is the 'violent teacher' that unleashes the destructive power of Man.

Thucydides, however, also wanted to raise awareness of the suffering that war always inflicts on the people. A shocking example is the 'Melian dialogue' (5.84–116), which dramatically illustrates the negotiations between Athens and the island of Melos, which attempted to remain neutral in the conflict, and the Athenian polis' claim to total power.[84]

Obviously, the immutability of human nature and of man – especially in regard to the magnitude of man's inhumanity – is the core theme of Thucydides' work, which he demonstrated with concrete historical examples to be a permanent, time-independent feature of all events. This unreserved, cynical exposure of human nature is the 'usefulness' of Thucydides' historical work.

First Encounter

The gate in the outer wall was not locked. I went through and knocked on the door. A moment passed before a drowsy, female voice called out:

'Who's there? We're sleeping!'

'Xenophon of Athens, rider in Critias' guard, in service of our Hipparchus Lysimachus. I would speak with Thucydides, son of Olorus.'

I avoided saying: 'I have orders to escort Thucydides to Critias.'

'I just told you – Thucydides is still sleeping.'

The deep, and in no way sleepy voice of a man rang out then: 'Who is it, Philesia? It's the middle of the night.'

'Xenophon from Athens. He wants to talk to you'

'Who? At this time of night?'

'Apparently so,' replied Philesia.

I was afraid that he would simply send me away, but then he called out:

'Well what does he want to talk to me about? Ask him, Philesia'

'You heard him Xenophon – out with it!' she demanded, impatient.

'I can only tell Thucydides himself, in private.'

Thucydides obviously wanted the matter dealt with quickly so he could return to bed. 'Was I away so long that I didn't notice how much the customs have changed? Used to be you'd leave your visits at least until mid-morning. Well, let the man in, Philesia!'

'You don't need a little more time..?'

'No, let's get this over with. Go back to bed.'

At that moment, the door opened. I looked into the blue eyes of a young woman. Judging by her light blonde hair, she was Thracian. Thucydides surely must have brought her with him from Skapte Hyle, I thought.[85]

He stood immediately behind her. He moved the young woman aside with a gentle hand movement. The strain of a long journey was evident in his face – he had only returned from Thrace two days ago. I had expected a bitter old man, but he was handsome, with fine features, his eyes open and friendly.

I introduced myself again. He interrupted me gently: 'I know who you are, Xenophon – you're a loyal follower of the men who allowed my return to Athens, the men who provided me with this house. Let's get to straight to the point.'

'I'm sorry Thucydides. I have been ordered to bring you to Critias immediately.'

'Ah! Dear Critias. I haven't seen him in an age – I wanted to visit him and give him my thanks. Good thing you came, then! But why at such an early hour? Why is he in such a hurry?'

I told him everything I had overheard the evening before. Thucydides was suddenly pale. Did he grasp the gravity of the situation? Did he realize how much danger he was in? The Thirty made short work of people they took a dislike to. Should I tell him to pack the essentials and take the fastest route out of the city? He saw my confusion. I asked quietly. 'Do you have friends in the city you can rely on?'

'Young man, do you want to be accused of not having done your job? Do you not know what that would mean for you? It wouldn't be as bad for me – Critias and I have known each other for so long! Go back to him and just tell him I had been meaning to visit him. But why the hurry?' he mumbled to himself. 'I won't run from him.'

'The Thirty are unpredictable,' I replied. 'They could ask you to leave Athens – willingly, obviously, or so they'll claim – or have you arrested.'

'Impossible! What for? I've only been here two days, and I'm not about to leave again. Besides, the journey is not one to be undertaken lightly. If they only knew how hard it is! So many boxes and baskets with all my books and papers! Completely out of the question! And the weather's not exactly favourable right now, either!'

There was a sharp, impatient knock at the door.

'What now?'

'We have to go, Xenophon!' Leontychus and Crinippus had grown tired of waiting.

I tried to buy time to gather my thoughts. What was I supposed to do? First, I calmed my comrades at the door: 'Thucydides is an old man and it's early – he needs time to wake up properly.'

'Fine. How much longer?'

'Just a little longer. Aren't the pubs open yet? It's getting light – go have a drink or something.'

'Good, we're practically frozen solid out here. Even so, you have to hurry up.'

One problem was solved for the time being. But how could I get Thucydides to see the danger he was in and leave his house and get to safety? It seemed hopeless – he was incapable of properly assessing the situation. He just wanted to return to his warm bed. So he called the Thracian woman and asked her to escort me out. He quickly said goodbye and returned to his bedroom. Then, suddenly, to my surprise, he came back out.

'I've changed my mind. I will go with the young man to see Critias, Philesia. What's the issue? Shut the door. Xenophon looks like he's seen a ghost. What harm could Critias do me?'

Suddenly, Philesia was crying: 'Please don't go. Let's just go to the harbour and go back to Thrace. You have lots of friends there – they love and idolize you.'

Her outburst affected me deeply. She was very afraid. Even I could hear those words echoing menacingly in my head from behind the door the night before: he must be silenced. Did that not mean they wanted to kill him? But how could I persuade this man, who was finally prepared to leave his house, not to visit Critias, but instead to flee to safety? At once, I was determined not to bring him to Critias. It would not be a happy reunion, I feared. He might not even get to *see his old friend. He would disappear into a prison somewhere, perhaps be delivered straight to the executioner. Lysimachus – the enforcer, as he was called – would see to that. The Thirty could rely on his unwavering obedience.*

I didn't consider for a moment that I would be putting myself in great danger by acting on my intentions. I was preoccupied with only one thought: how could I get Thucydides to safety? Especially as I would first have to dissuade him from accepting Critias' invitation, which I had brought to him myself. Then a life-saving thought – or so I believed then – came to me. I let Philesia in on the secret first, while Thucydides was busy hunting for a scroll he wanted to bring Critias as a gift.

Then I spoke to him, quietly, but emphatically: 'Thucydides. Let's let Critias wait a while longer. Can't you take a little detour? Come visit my father Gryllus' house for few hours! Our farm is very close to the city, it's not far at all.'

Philesia, on cue, came out of the kitchen and exclaimed with excitement: 'Yes please! Let's take Xenophon up on his kind offer!' It would be easy to get to a harbour from our farm unnoticed and catch a ship to Thrace, I had told Philesia.

Whether or not Thucydides saw through this plan at the time, I never found out. He could at least not ignore the fact that his girlfriend wanted to return to Thrace with him as soon as possible. He nodded silently. After all, he wanted to see my father again, whom he knew from a previous life.

I didn't need to explain the way to our farm. As if fearing that something bad would happen, he asked only that I send a reliable man to his house as soon as possible to pick up some of his records.

My father worked on our land in the plains of Cephissus himself. He was proud when people referred to him as an 'auturgus' –a farmer – who cultivated his own fields. He certainly could have confined himself to organising the work on our farm, but he always wanted to lend a hand, believing – as his old friend Ischomachus was forever trying to convince Socrates – that smart farming is the source of all virtues. Socrates, however, was not ready to venture into the land beyond the city walls 'because the trees had nothing to teach him'.[86]

Life on the Farm

In his writings on the management of a farm, the *Oeconomicus*, Xenophon explains in detail that successful agriculture is based on a well-organised relationship between man and woman, and a loving trust. He presents here a stark contrast to the relationship of disrespectful rudeness between Socrates and his wife Xanthippe. He doesn't only describe the possibilities for a productive division of labour between the sexes, however. 'In the same way as the Persian nobleman is a combination of soldier and farmer, so throughout the dialogue Xenophon implies that the lessons taught by farming are the same as those taught by soldiering. … The blend of ability and devotion of farmer and soldier is Xenophon's educational ideal.'[87]

In this, he is no different from Aristophanes, whose wine-farmer Trygaeus – in his play *Peace*, premièred in 421 BC – praised his idyllic country life.[88] In the midst of the Peloponnesian war, the comedy writer presented a peaceful utopia: 'Men, remember the happy life of the past that Peace made possible. Think of the preserved fruits, the figs, the myrtle berries, the sweet cider, the violets at the spring, and the olives, of which we are so fond. Thank the goddess for these blessings.'

Xenophon's pleasant view of rural life did not, however, get lost in the inaccessibility of eternal peace. He viewed hard work on the farm as the best preparation for war, which – like Thucydides – he held to be Man's essential mode of being.

Aristophanes has Trygaeus fly to the heavens to visit Zeus, whom he begs to end the raging Peloponnesian war. The farmer's flying machine is a huge dung beetle. He achieves his objective. However, every last one of the gods, down to Hermes, withdraws, and leaves the Greek people to Polemos (the divine embodiment of War), who has imprisoned Eirene, goddess of Peace, in a pit. Trygaeus is forced to watch as War tosses Greek cities and the products of their labour into a mortar, where they are to be ground up. Luckily, however, he has forgotten to bring a pestle. The wine-farmer uses this time to summon Greeks from all tribes to help rescue Peace from the pit before War finds his pestle. The goddess of Peace is freed. At the end of the play, the farmer is able to reap his harvest in the form of Opora, a beautiful young woman. Arms manufacturers are ruined and the producers of agricultural implements see a massive increase in sales.

When the comedy premièred, the Peloponnesian war had been raging for ten years. A few days after the first performance, the so-called Peace of Nicias, which was supposed to last for fifty years, began. It was, however, only brief.

Gryllus' Farm

Of course we had excellent stalls for sheep, goats and pigs, and large pastures, which we needed for our very successful horse-breeding trade. The great Alcibiades once even won in the Olympics – twelve years before the end of the Great War – with a team of horses bred by my father.[89]

The war had left its mark on our farm. Our vines and olive trees had been partially wiped out in the great Pericles' attempts to make a fortress out of Athens and Piraeus. The farmers were to find shelter in the city, while the surrounding land was surrendered to the enemy. Despite the enemy's attacks, Gryllus had not heeded Pericles' call. He explained again and again, full of pride, how he was not locked up between the Long Walls like the Acharnians, but defending his own land against the ravages of the enemy with his own hands. He was so successful that in Athens it was said the Spartans had purposefully spared my father – an opportunity for many rumours. Gryllus had merely hit upon an effective means of protecting his land. He had underground tunnels dug, natural depressions and caves covered and camouflaged, artificial barriers built that forced the enemy to change their marching direction. In this way, he managed to hide his fields and – more importantly – his sheds and barns from the enemy.

Because he refused to starve between the Long Walls, as he put it, Gryllus was involved in numerous small surprise attacks against the enemy, who suffered significant losses as a result. Precise knowledge of the terrain gave our people a great advantage, of course. It was also our own land, and we weren't going to give it up without a fight. My father always spoke with great pride about his dangerous missions, led by Pericles himself, who supported the missions with whatever means possible.[90]

Around this time, there was a brief cavalry engagement at Phrygioi, in which the Athenian division, to which my father belonged, clashed with the Boeotian cavalry. The Athenians were supported by Thessalian horsemen. Only when the Boeotians arrived to help with their armoured troops did the Athenians and Thessalians have to retreat. Their dead and wounded were left behind. Gryllus would acknowledge this defeat, but would always remind whoever would listen that the Peloponnesians had only won with the help of the Boeotian hoplites, which was probably true.

Although re-cultivating the grapevines would take time, and it would be ten years before the first fruits could be shaken down from a young olive tree, we were quite lucky in the circumstances. Our stud farm remained untouched. Whenever the enemy troops came near, we brought the horses into a spacious rock-cut cellar, which we could close with a large wooden gate. The gate was, in turn, completely covered with a huge, mobile thorny hedge. This was an ingenious invention of my father's, which also served to protect against horse thieves in more peaceful times. The lush rose bushes were rooted in large wooden boxes, which could be moved back and forth on wheels. The bush was so dense that it served its purpose even during winter when the leaves had fallen. The roses were originally from my mother's rose garden, which she had tended as long as she lived with equal competence and devotion. We always had the most beautiful flowers for both public and private occasions.

When I talked Thucydides into seeking refuge on our farm, I was unaware that I was putting not only myself and Thucydides, but also my father, in grave danger. Critias, through his extensive network of spies, was aware of our every move in detail. He knew full well that Thucydides would not get far if he tried to leave Athens secretly, as it would be impossible to find a ship to Thrace at short notice and load it with his belongings quickly and quietly.

Of course, Critias and his people were well aware that my father had effectively turned his property into a fortress during the war, where one could easily hide out. He could also expect that Gryllus would readily be able to send a carriage to Athens carrying Thucydides to the harbour. It was obviously clear to him that I would plan and undertake this with great care. He had considered everything from the beginning. He, the leader of the Thirty, was apparently prepared to let his childhood friend Thucydides fall into a trap. It was a perfidious game, which I was playing without even realising it. I had completely pushed the thought that Critias was the leader of this brutal regime out of my head. It didn't occur to me that he was only using me to eliminate Thucydides and – I realised much later – get his hands on Thucydides' controversial archives.

This strategy resembles Odysseus' scheme to bring the disabled Philoctetes to Troy, for an old oracle had prophesied that the city could only be conquered with the arrows of Hercules, who had given his bow to Philoctetes for lighting the pyre on which Hercules was to die. Our great Sophocles had written a tragedy around this old story. I was just sixteen when my father took me to a performance of Philoctetes at a theatre in Athens. At the time, I had no idea that six years later I would play a role in real life similar to the young Neoptolemus, the son of Achilles in Sophocles' tragedy.

Philoctetes

Sophocles' *Philoctetes* premièred in Athens in 409 BC. The Greeks learned only in the tenth year of their siege that Troy could only be conquered by Hercules' arrows. Agamemnon and Menelaus, however, had forced Philoctetes to settle on the island of Lemnos, for his festering foot exuded an unbearable stench. He had been bitten by a snake, leaving him with a wound that would not heal. He was in great pain, and no one could endure the screams of his suffering. Now, however, he was needed as a saviour. He lived alone on the island. Of course, he could not forgive what the House of Atreus had done to him.

Odysseus assesses the situation and devises a scheme. He is accompanied by Neoptolemus, the son of Achilles. Neoptolemus will use his moral integrity in the scheme to serve the interests of the Greeks – he is to tell the bitter old man that he has been cheated out of his father's weapons, and that he is therefore returning to Greece. Philoctetes will then ask to be taken with him. As soon as Philoctetes has boarded the ship, he will be overpowered and taken to Troy.

At first, everything goes according to plan. Philoctetes comes to trust Neoptolemus, who is forced to tell the old man the truth. Deeply hurt, Philoctetes no longer wishes to board the ship. Finally, Hercules, now a god, intervenes and tells Philoctetes to go to Troy and end the war.

Guilt

Since the banishment of the Thirty to Eleusis,[91] fifteen extremely exciting years had passed,[92] and the world première of Philoctetes was more than twenty years ago. For a long time, I could not let go of the question of whether or not I had been responsible for the death of Thucydides. Had I really been the clueless tool of Critias, as Neoptolemus had been the tool of the cunning Odysseus? Did I gain Thucydides' confidence through trickery in order to deliver him, unsuspecting, to his enemies? I know – every comparison has its limits. But what sets me apart from the son of Achilles only makes matters worse. Neoptolemus was used for a noble cause – to win the war against Troy. But me? Thucydides' death and the destruction of his property will never have been a noble cause. Neoptolemus was able to ask Philoctetes for forgiveness for his unintentional breach of trust. I, however, never had the slightest chance of revealing a monstrous fraud and atoning. My only consolation was that I had lied without even knowing it. Pious Sophocles brought everything to a happy ending. He had the divine Hercules intervene and provide a solution. Where was Hercules when Thucydides' life was in need of saving?

I hoped at the time that Thucydides would accept my invitation to visit my father's farm, never expecting him to agree with such astonishing speed. Of course, I didn't know what he was thinking. Now, I think he had never intended to leave his home town again. Even Philesia, who was achingly homesick, probably could not have been persuaded to board the ship to Thrace.

Meanwhile, the sun was already quite high. It was time. I had to expect that Lysimachus, the enforcer, had been sent after us to find out why we had not fulfilled his orders.

However, like Hercules, Lysimachus had apparently forgotten us. Even my comrades Leontychus and Crinippus had disappeared, determined to get caught in a wine shop somewhere. For officers of the Thirty, we could be an undisciplined and unreliable lot!

I was able to leave Thucydides' house inconspicuously to fetch a carriage. It wasn't long before I was successful. The driver promised to deliver the writer and the young Thracian woman safely to our farm.

That evening, I wanted to meet. The route would take half an hour by horse. How was I supposed to explain to Lysimachus why we had returned without Thucydides? I had not told my two friends, but I couldn't just tell them he wasn't at home – they had heard and seen him when he came to the door at dawn. So I claimed the writer had escaped secretly through the small backyard. Philesia had briefly distracted me so I wouldn't notice the man disappearing. I wanted to appear contrite, and repentant for my alleged failure. Of course it was all invented – down to the enchanting effect Philesia had on me.

To my surprise, Lysimachus no longer showed any interest in Thucydides. Obviously, the case was settled for him. He gave no further orders. I couldn't figure out what it meant. In the early morning, I rode to my father's farm. When I arrived, the two men were engaged in a stimulating conversation. The two had just had dinner, and Charicleia, my father's housekeeper, was busy tidying away the leftovers with Philesia's help. Everything seemed to be in order and the excitement of the day was forgotten. Gryllus and Thucydides were happy to see me, waving as I tended to my horse and brought it into the barn. That my father was happy to see me was no surprise, but Thucydides? Why was he so cheerful? Did he think he was safe? Did he really believe that Critias had no idea where he was? He had spies everywhere. The fact that I had spent an evening and a night at home didn't seem to have aroused any suspicion. I only had to return to Athens in time the next morning. I could be counted on to do that – I took my duties very seriously.

Insubordination

Only once was there an incident of any note.[93] The democratic general Thrasybulus had organised several campaigns to free the city from the Thirty. The situation was very tense.[94] We riders spent even the nights together with our horses out in the odeon.[95] Of course there were no musical performances at the time, but the pavilion roof of the building built by Pericles afforded us some protection from the cold and the rain.

We had orders to patrol the rubble of the long walls on foot and on horseback from the early morning until late at night. We expected an attack by the democrats from Piraeus – they had been arming themselves with increased fervour lately, and had been undertaking brief raids again to stock up on food. We had been tasked with taking 'decisive action' against the looters. It was while we were doing this that we encountered a handful of people from Aixone, a demos on the coast south of Athens. They were trying to find food. Our hipparchus gave us the order to slaughter them. They were unarmed and begged for their lives.[96] We refused to carry out the shameful command. We protested loudly. Lysimachus was furious. He was powerless, unable even to invoke a higher power, as he would usually do in tricky situations, as the Thirty had long since fled to Eleusis. Critias and

Hippomachus – and many other supporters of the Thirty – had already died in the fight against the men from Piraeus.[97] General confusion prevailed, and there was deep distrust everywhere. As a result, Lysimachus didn't dare to bring us to account for his shameful order.

But I am getting well ahead of myself. That night, at least, when Thucydides was our guest, Critias still possessed unlimited power – his death was just a few weeks away. He was sure that Thucydides could not harm him while he was staying with my father. However, there were crates and baskets of his papers still at his house in the city, unattended and unsupervised. This remained the case for some time.

It had cost him a fortune – Thucydides was telling my father – to get the information for his work of history. 'I lived in Thrace for eight years after the war,'[98] said Thucydides, 'unwillingly, very far from the centres of power, as you know.'

I didn't know this. I had only heard that Thucydides had served as strategist for Thrace in Amphipolis. I thought he had settled there in order to be able to better supervise the workers in his gold mines. So I asked: 'Why unwillingly?'

My father gave me a stern look and shook his head disapprovingly. I shouldn't press the issue.

Thucydides did not miss my father's look. 'Never mind, Gryllus! The boy's just curious.'

Then he told me how, after he had recovered from the plague which had killed so many in Athens at the beginning of the war, he had been appointed strategist.[99]

Amphipolis

In winter of the eighth year of the war,[100] the Lacedaemonian Brasidas was granted permission by the Spartan leaders to carry out a military campaign in the Chalcidian-Thracian area. He was hailed throughout Greece as the liberator of Athens, having achieved considerable military success with his mercenaries and helots, and was planning to advance on Amphipolis on the River Strymon.[101] He advanced on the ill-prepared city under cover of night, supported by numerous residents of the surrounding countryside. Because of the inclement weather, no one expected a raid. Without significant resistance, Brasidas occupied the entire area before the city.

There was great panic in Amphipolis itself. The Spartans were ready to take the city at a moment's notice. The Spartan sympathisers in the city, however, were not able to open the gates to the enemy, and the Athenian garrison commander refused to surrender. He immediately sent a message to Thucydides asking for help. Thucydides was half a day away from Amphipolis, with his warships near the island of Thasos.

Thucydides took seven ships and set sail as quickly as possible. The operation was, however, doomed from the start. Except for rowers and helmsmen, there were only seventy soldiers – just ten on each ship – between the seven triremes, and half of those were Thracian archers who couldn't be trusted in the slightest. They would certainly not fight against their own countrymen. Thucydides had perhaps thirty reliable men, and would have had no chance against the powerful Spartan units.

He also failed to reach Amphipolis on time, and was only able to secure the port of Eion.[102] In the grand scheme of things, however, the campaign was inconsequential to the outcome of the war. Brasidas had nothing to fear from seven ill-equipped ships. In Thucydides, however, he saw an influential owner of gold mines, and one of the most powerful men on the Thracian mainland. He was afraid, therefore, that Thucydides would be able to recruit more troops in the long run with his financial resources to help support the city.

On the Responsibility of the Gods

I believed Thucydides' failure to be the will of the gods, because they wanted to save him from a mission that was as dangerous as it was pointless. The writer smiled kindly at my remark: 'It's not as simple as that, my dear Xenophon. If it were, I would have to assume that my exile was also willed by the gods, and I'm not so sure of that. We can't blame the gods for everything. Usually, men are to blame for their own misfortune.'

'So our poet said,' interjected Gryllus, and quoted the words of the father of the gods and of men, as written by Homer:[103] 'Look you now, how ready mortals are to blame the gods. It is from us, they say, that evils come, but they even of themselves, through their own blind folly, have sorrows beyond that which is ordained.'

My father certainly never intended to offend Thucydides with this quote, nor to indicate his guilt in the Amphipolis disaster. I, too, had only wanted to say that I believed his banishment for Amphipolis was grossly unjust, because the gods themselves are ultimately responsible for everything. At the time, however, I had only an inkling of the role the gods played in the operation in question. Only in my later life did I see with my own eyes again and again that divine power did not lose its grip on the reins in both the large as well as the small events.[104] Many events can be attributed, with good reason, to the intervention of the gods.[105]

'Brasidas was a brilliant strategist, and far superior to me,' said Thucydides. 'My campaign was doomed to failure.' Sighing, he added: 'Nearly two years later,

he was defeated at Amphipolis by a much stronger opponent[106]*: He defeated Cleon and his resting Athenian forces, but was gravely wounded. He received word that his troops had been successful before finally succumbing.*[107]

'Cleon fell in this battle, too' interjected Gryllus.

'No, not in the battle,' replied Thucydides. 'He was hit in the head by a stone thrown by a slinger from Myrkinos as he fled.'

'And then?' I asked impatiently. Thucydides ignored my question.

'The Lacedaemonian Brasidas was buried with full honours, and with many condolences from our allies. He was even granted a grave in the middle of the city. To this day, the inhabitants of Amphipolis bring him sacrifices and organise festivals to honour him as a hero of legend every year. The Amphipolitans see him as the saviour of their city,' added my father, who had heard the story of Brasidas' exploits again and again during his travels to Sparta in the years of the peace of Nicias.[108]

'Falling to such a foe is a great honour in itself,' I ventured.

'For twenty years, I have consoled myself with that exact thought, my friend, but Brasidas wasn't all I had to contend with. I also had to deal with the especially devastating power politics of my own countrymen, the Athenians. Understandable that our enemies hated us, more than feared us. Amphipolis is just another more or less insignificant example of those misguided, inhuman Athenian power politics.'

Socrates had also fought at Amphipolis as a hoplite under Cleon, I thought, and at the same time, the thought suddenly occurred to me that the revered philosopher had therefore put his life on the line for these 'inhuman' politics, as he had at Delion[109] and Potidea[110] before the war had even properly begun. Then I heard Thucydides say: 'I can imagine what you're thinking, Xenophon, but I don't blame Socrates for fulfilling his duties as an Athenian hoplite. Quite the opposite – he dedicated his life as a brave soldier to his home city, without being able to influence the course of history. Then his voice took on a hard edge: 'But we must not forget what our fellow citizens were doing to the Melians in the summer of the sixteenth year of the war.[111] Our people explained this at the time by urging us to consider what the victor would do with us if we were defeated,[112] should they wish to take revenge on us for our crimes. My historical work shows what happened back then, but I'm not even happy with my version of events. Perhaps I will contrive two speeches discussing the opposing viewpoints. That would make the background to the events more accessible. Socrates surely wouldn't begrudge me trying to imitate him and allow the Athenians and Melians to have a dialogue. What do you think? It's all still up in the air.'

'I think it sounds like an excellent idea to make the opposing views easy to understand like that,' I interjected boldly.

'Well, when I get back to work, I will think more on it, my dear Xenophon, that I promise you,' said Thucydides with a smile. Sadly, he would only partially fulfil his promise to present the events at Melos in detail.

'Can I ask you about something else?' I said. 'Couldn't the war have ended after ten years, when Cleon and Brasidas were dead?'

'Exactly. Both sides were exhausted. They wanted peace. To be more precise: with Brasidas and Cleon dead, the war could have finally ended then. They were the ones who fought most fiercely against peace – Brasidas for military glory, Cleon, to prevent his crimes and atrocities from being discovered after a peace treaty.[113] Only once, perhaps because Cleon and Brasidas were no longer part of the equation, were Pleistoanax, son of Pausanias, and Nicias able to hold peace talks and come to an agreement[114] after ten summers and ten winters. I will deal with all of this in my book, of course.'

Xenophon's *Hellenica*

In his work, Xenophon describes the history of Greece from 411 BC to 362 BC. The first part (1–2.3.10) covers the period up to the end of the Peloponnesian war (404 BC). The second part (2.3.11–7) covers the period up to the Battle of Mantinea (363 BC). 'The close connection between books I and II of *Hellenica* and Thucydides' work has always been a subject of speculation […].'[115] According to Diogenes Laërtius (2.57), Xenophon published and publicised Thucydides' work, the assumption being that Xenophon used Thucydides' material for the first two books of his *Hellenica*. Although no hard evidence for this exists, it is a possibility that should not be completely ruled out. It is quite conceivable that Xenophon – even though he apparently began work on his 'sequel' long after the death of Thucydides – made use of Thucydides' material.

After the description of the end of the war, the *Hellenica* reports on the rule of the Thirty Tyrants and their deposition (2.3.11–2.4), before moving onto the Spartan conflict with Persia in the years 401 BC to 386 BC, and simultaneous events in the motherland (3.1–5.1). In 5.2–7.27, the climax and the fall of Spartan power is described, as well as the rise of Thebes and the Battle of Mantinea in the year 362 BC.

In Xenophon's work, Greek history is thus reduced to the history of Sparta after the end of the Peloponnesian war. One reason for this imbalance likely lies in the fact that Xenophon based his work primarily on personal observations and recollections he had collected as a companion to the Spartan king Agesilaus. He seems not to have used any other material besides his own records, although he had access to sources of information in Athens from the beginning of the 360s.

In the first two books, Xenophon attempts to imitate Thucydides' style as closely as possible. He adopts Thucydides' chronology, and tries to adapt his style to that of his predecessor. Besides private records and eyewitness accounts, he likely used a work on local Athenian history known as an 'Atthis'.

A central theme of Xenophon's work[116] is the decline Sparta experienced after the victory in the Peloponnesian war. The loss of power is, in Xenophon's eyes, due to the gods' anger at Sparta for breaking its oath to allow Greek cities to retain their autonomy.

Obviously, Xenophon depended less on comprehensive historiographical representation and analysis of historical events. He especially wanted to portray 'glorious deeds', without paying attention to their historical importance in a wider context.[117] His goal was to highlight the quintessential importance of human performance, regardless of its historical impact. Additionally, he depended on vivid portrayals of personalities whose deeds meant they stood out from the crowd. This interest is also evident in his other writings (in particular Agesilaus and the Cyropaedia).[118]

Fear for Thucydides

One morning, as I saddled my horse, I turned to find Philesia standing beside me. She looked at me, serious and sad. Abruptly, in a low voice, as though she wanted not to be heard, she said: 'Xenophon, yesterday Thucydides received a letter. He said "Tomorrow, I have to return to Athens, Critias has summoned me again – he's serious this time. He must have something important to discuss". I couldn't keep it to myself, Xenophon. I'm scared something has happened to Thucydides. What should I do?'

I was speechless. The brief pleasure I had felt in seeing Philesia suddenly standing before me had disappeared immediately. I was dismayed, although I had suspected that the beautiful days spent on our farm would not last forever. 'Thucydides has made his decision. He can't be dissuaded. He won't let anyone stop him from going to Critias,' I said simply, before riding off.

Philesia was silent. She seemed to agree with me – she knew him better than anyone, after all. Why that was, I only discovered some time later.

A strange unrest had seized the city. It meant we had to be prepared for anything. Lysimachus immediately forbade us from leaving the city. Uprisings were expected, perhaps even a civil war. A terrible possibility. Rumours circulated that the rule of the Thirty was at an end. The people on the street were silent as we approached, regarding us with hostility. As usual, I had no idea why. I was

more concerned with the health of my horse than with the political situation.
Before, we had always been greeted with joy, even jubilation, and we were proud
of it. But if the rule of the Thirty was really over, then what had Critias wanted
with Thucydides? Did he want to protect him from the radical democrats, like
Cleon? Cleon had many followers even now, even though he had died long ago.

Cleon and Diodotus

Cleon, son of Cleainetus, was a leather producer, and owner of a tannery
in Athens. Politically, he distinguished himself as a radical democrat and
passionate opponent of Pericles. After Pericles' death, Cleon made his mark
as a leader of men alongside the cloth merchant Eucrates and the sheep
trader Lysicles. Thucydides[119] described him as the 'most violent man'[120] in
the city, with the greatest influence over the people. For Thucydides, Cleon
was the epitome of the demagogue who pretended to represent the interests
of the people, but was pursuing only his own goals.

This negative image of Cleon depicted by Thucydides can also,
incidentally, be found in Aristophanes' play *The Knights*, in which Cleon
appears as a Paphlagonian slave.[121] This paints a striking portrait of Cleon,
to the point that no actor wanted to take his role, and the poet himself had
to play the Paphlagonian.[122] A year earlier, Aristophanes had let the choir in
The Acharnians explain how he was looking forward to flaying Cleon and
using his skin to make sandals for the knights.

After Cleon met his end in the battle against the Spartan Brasidas –
according to Thucydides[123] – his crimes became known, and his words
proved to be nothing more than malevolent warmongering.

When the city of Mytilene on the island of Lesbos seceded from Athens
in the year 427 BC, but was recaptured by Paches, Cleon, in Athens, called
for the execution of all able-bodied men and the enslavement of the women
and children in Mytilene. A decision was made by the people's assembly, but
withdrawn in the wake of a speech by Diodotus, son of Eucrates.[124] Instead,
around 1,000 aristocrats – the leaders of the betrayal against Athens – were
executed.[125]

In his speech, the otherwise unknown Diodotus reproaches Cleon for
'dazzling listeners and naysayers with suspicions. Athens needs speakers,
and it needs objective discussion between them, free of slander. This
encourages more study of the thing in question, with more thoroughness
and foresight than listeners are capable of. They, however, are subject to a

different responsibility than the speakers. When something goes wrong, Athenians punish he who instigated the thing, rather than he who did it. So, to the point: the death penalty deters no one – desire and hope will bring people together again and again at risk to themselves. But if the Athenians were to execute the entire population in addition to those actually guilty of seceding, they would have no one left on whom to count. Finally, the people of Mytilene only went through with secession under coercion, and once they had weapons in their hands, they surrendered the city to the Athenians.'[126]

For Diodotus,[127] Cleon embodied the opposite of a clear mind. He accuses him – indirectly – of hasty action and anger, commonly associated with stupidity, lack of intelligence or mental limitations. Whoever dismisses speeches as irrelevant to action, Diodotus claims, was either unreasonable or selfish: a man is unreasonable when he says he could discuss the future, or uncertainties, in another way; a man is pursuing his own personal interests when he plans something shameful and says he can't argue for corruption, but is fully prepared to intimidate his listeners and opponents with slander. The ideal politician must try to prove that his arguments are the strongest on the same level as his opponent – fair interaction is only possible under these conditions.

After this preamble, Diodotus explains that everything he says is about the city of Athens' advantage, and nothing more. One must always keep the city's advantage in mind. The same applies to the death penalty, which has no empirical deterrent effect. Even if you have the law on your side, you should be more ready to accept injustice than to kill someone who may be useful for the city if kept alive.

After Diodotus' speech, discussion raged until the principle of usefulness prevailed, and it was decided – in opposition to Cleon – that the population of Mytilene would be left unharmed, except for the 'main culprits'.

Might and Right

A few years later, however, the Athenians had all men on the Island of Melos killed, because they would not submit to the enslavement of their women and children, and the distribution of their sparsely populated land among Athenian citizens. In Thucydides' work, the Melians negotiate with an Athenian embassy to avert disaster.[128] This situation would have benefited from a man such as Diodotus, who might have persuaded the Athenians to behave more reasonably. The Athenians declared from the outset that there would be no discussion between Athens and Melos regarding whether they were acting lawfully or not.

In the *Melian Dialogue*, Thucydides did not want to give an example of – or even criticize – the idea, mooted by the sophists, of 'might makes right'. He simply states that it is in the nature of man that 'the strong rule over the weak',[129] but that this law applies only among equals.[130] The strong enforce what they can; the weak must submit without a fight.

The Athenians had unlimited power. The subjugation of the Melians was a foregone conclusion – it was only a matter of how the Melians would deal with their situation. They could submit, or they could die.

Thucydides is far from being able to judge the arguments of the Athenians in conversation with the Melians. He has the Athenians explain that they couldn't have acted in any other way: 'We believe that, compelled by their very nature, the gods may and men do rule wherever they are able. We did not make this rule, nor are we the first to have acted on it in the time it has existed. We merely make use of it. We found it already in existence before us, and shall leave it to exist forever after us. We know that you, and every other man, having the same power as we have, would do the same as we do.' (5.105.2).

However, there are reasonable limits for even the powerful – the principle of utility that dominated the debate about the measures against the people of Mytilene requires that self-indulgence be abandoned. To do so, 'calm thought' is required,[131] preventing wrong decisions from being made. Diodotus pointed out that the conflict with Mytilene was not about right and wrong – irrelevant variables in the study of history in Thucydides' eyes – but about actions on the grounds of 'reasonable consideration', which are only useful for the actor in the long run[132]: 'We are not in a court of justice, and the question is not what is right, but how the Mitylenians might be useful to us.'[133]

Diodotus feared that the Athenians would lose sight of utility if moderation were forgotten. 'It is necessary for us to judge people who have made a mistake and who have surely harmed us by doing so, but rather see how by moderate punishment we might in future give the cities the opportunity to be of use to us; we must be careful that we achieve what we desire not through the severity of the law, but through proper treatment.'[134]

In the Melian dialogue, the Athenians recognise the reason for moderation – for the sake of utility, they point out their 'moderate offer', which they demand the Melians accept. The Athenians add to this a pragmatic statement on intergovernmental relations: 'Those who do not yield to their equals, who respect their superiors and are moderate towards their inferiors, on the whole succeed best'.[135]

Assumptions about a Missing Epilogue

Even in the lead-up to the Peloponnesian war, the Athenians made it obvious to the Spartans that they felt obligated towards moderation: 'It should be praised that we dominate others as is human nature, but respect justice more than our position compels us to. We imagine that our moderation would be best demonstrated by the conduct of others who should be placed in our position. Even our equity has unreasonably subjected us to condemnation instead of approval.'[136]

In the case of Melos, the Athenians did not uphold the principle of proper moderation in order to achieve utility in the long run.

Even though Xenophon's *Hellenica* continues Thucydides' work from the exact point it leaves off, there remains the possibility that Thucydides himself had already planned an epilogue to attempt to clarify the questions surrounding the cause of the Athenian defeat. He would have been able to continue his reflections on 'proper moderation'. 'It may be suggested that in the parts of the works that Thucydides had not yet written, it would have been shown that the situation in 416 BC was not actually and ultimately about the Melian decision, but rather that the Athenians had made the wrong decision long before the negotiations – insofar as this decision was based on an incorrect assessment of the actual ξύμφορον, that, through political myopia, had only considered the immediate benefit, and not the necessary damage in the far future that would result from their actions. Losing sight of proper moderation prevented the realisation that it was precisely political measures such as those taken against Melos that had a major role in the isolation of Athens, and its ultimate downfall. In 427 BC, this μετριάζειν had not yet been lost'.[137]

Utility or advantage is acceptable as the desired result of action when associated with the proper moderation.[138] That may also have been Thucydides' own point of view: he urges Man to observe proper moderation in the realisation of their own ξύμφορον: it is a mandatory standard for a statesman to confirm to and align μετριάζειν and μέτρον in his decisions'.[139] With sophrosyne, the ability to recognise the proper moderation and prudence, he can make this happen.

Thucydides and the Cleonists

It was no secret that Thucydides deeply despised the unscrupulous Cleon and was privately amused that the learned tanner was mocked by the comedy writer – even though he had been dead for twenty years! What could he do to the historian now? Absolutely nothing.

But there were many others like Cleon: Cleonists, as I called them. As an aristocrat, Thucydides was, to some extent, their natural enemy. His book no doubt contained many embarrassing truths about Cleon. The humiliating defeat of the demagogues and their flight from the Spartan Brasidas was an example Thucydides was particularly fond of.[140] Critias was also aware of this fact. So I was thankful that he – at least I assumed – was reaching out to protect Thucydides. Critias' days in Athens, however, were numbered. As a result, there was nothing he could do for the historian but suggest for a second time that he leave Athens and escape from the radical democrats.

What if the letter Philesia had mentioned was a forgery that had not come from Critias, though? Then someone wanted to lure the historian into a deadly trap. Was his house already in the hands of the Cleonists? They had every reason to fear his revelations – his statements were backed up with thorough investigation and evidence. With a few strokes of his pen he had, for example, confirmed the image presented by Aristophanes and – worst of all – he had turned the comedy writer's mockery into bitterly serious historiography.

I didn't mention the possibility of a forged letter of invitation to Philesia. It would only upset her further.

It occurred to me, when she was standing beside me, that I had found a way out. The problem was that I had once seen Critias as a friend and ally, but that Philesia knew him only as a dangerous enemy. It would be pointless to explain to the young woman that she needn't be afraid. Even the prospect of returning to Thrace was no consolation. Until she knew Thucydides was safe, she could think of nothing else.

I worried that today would be the last day I saw him. So I asked Lysimachus to give me one more day off duty, despite the curfew. 'My father has fallen suddenly ill,' I lied. 'He wants me to watch over him tonight.'

Of course, Gryllus was fine. He was never ill. He even tolerated the unexpected death of my mother Diodora last year relatively well. So it seemed, anyway. Whenever I asked how he was, he always answered the same way: 'I still have old Charicleia. She takes care of the house for me, kind old soul,' he smiled, and added, 'Of course, maybe my son will find me a hard-working daughter-in-law soon. Everything will be different once there are grandchildren to look after anyway.'

Sadly, he did not live to see that. He died suddenly while working the fields. I was already on the way to Cyrus. The news caught up with me in Ephesus.

Years later, one of our former servants told me that Gryllus had kept hold of the heavy plough, even in death. The mules stood motionless in the half-ploughed acre where he was found, not moving from their spots. They were waiting, as usual, for their master's command.

The strong old man had hardly even slumped over when he died. Only his upper body was slightly inclined forward. The animals actually seemed thankful for the unexpected break, the former servant said. The mules refused to move from their spot until Gryllus had been carried away on a stretcher. Whenever I think of that, that I was not at home when my father died, I am overcome with a deep, painful sadness. I couldn't even be there for his burial.

I had actually been home that night, but Lysimachus had ordered me to return by dawn the next morning. The situation was tense and unpredictable.

The sun was already up when I returned to the house. Oddly enough, Thucydides was waiting at the door for me. Gryllus was busy checking the bridle of the horse and carriage that was to take his guest to Athens the next morning. Thucydides asked me, in his words, for a brief conversation in private. I dismounted and left my sweating horse with Lykus, who had come running from the barn upon my arrival. I felt an unusual restlessness. Charicleia came towards me, tears in her eyes, and embraced me: 'Thank God you're here, my dear. We were so worried.'

'Why? I'm earlier than I said I'd be. What's wrong?'

'You haven't heard?'

'Heard what?'

'The city is in chaos – you must have noticed something!'

'No, Charicleia, everything seemed normal to me.'

'My God, you have to look after yourself!'

She turned from me quickly and shouted into the house: 'Where are you, Philesia? Have you packed everything yet?'

The young woman called back: 'Packed what? He'll be back no later than midday tomorrow, he doesn't need to take everything with him. He explicitly told me not to pack anything. His friend Critias will have everything he needs.'

When Thucydides came to me and greeted me formally, I sensed impatience in his voice: 'I must speak with you urgently, Xenophon. Walk with me a while – dinner isn't ready yet anyway.'

With these words, we fell into silence. Thucydides and I had never been alone together, I realised.

'Xenophon, as you know, I will be leaving tomorrow morning to meet Critias. He sent me an invitation yesterday. Actually, I'm delighted to hear from him again after so long. I can finally thank him for making my return to Athens possible after all these years.'

He then proceeded to give me a detailed lecture on the importance of gratitude. I was impressed. He spoke like a sophist, the effect of his words more important than the meaning. I had never seen him like this. But he made the desired impression – I felt terribly ungrateful. I imagined I had neglected gratitude my entire life. A horrible idea for me at the time, for whoever is ungrateful not only offends the gods, but his parents, and his country too! It was always said that ingratitude was shameless, and the cause of many crimes.[141]

Why was Thucydides talking about it now? What did he intend with this momentary agnonisma?[142] Did he want to demonstrate that he had also mastered the art of the sophists? That he was a good student of the famous Gorgias, with his antithetical statements, a Prodicus, with his ability to define ethical-political terms, and a Protagoras, with his brilliant proof technique? I thought back to my own rhetoric teaching, in which the great sophist enlightenment had been presented over and over as a shining example for us to follow.

Naturally, I asked him: 'Why are you talking about gratitude with such detail and verbosity? Are you trying to tell me I have been ungrateful to you?' He didn't answer.

Many years later, I got an explanation: Thucydides was afraid, and he was trying to drown his fear with words. That he chose this topic to discuss – as a diligent student of the sophists, he would be able to discuss any number of topics off the cuff – naturally had something to do with Critias. He was genuinely grateful to him. My visit a few days earlier on behalf of the Thirty, however, had troubled him more than he would admit. He knew full well he was now threatened on two fronts: by the Thirty, and by the Cleonists. He knew that the Thirty were losing their grip on power, and decided to accept Critias' invitation despite this fact, or maybe because of it. Did he really still believe he was friends with Critias? He was naturally very curious about everything the man was doing. He was, after all, a passionate historian and chronicler.

At the time, I suspected – as I said – that Critias wanted to eliminate Thucydides for reasons I was not privy to. His archive, of which Critias was surely aware, contained huge amounts of information that could be used against almost any political actor of the time. That was an unpleasant thought to the Thirty, as it was to the Cleonists and the moderate democrats.

The Coffer

Suddenly, I heard Thucydides saying: 'Let's get to the point, Xenophon. I need you to go to my house in Athens while I'm visiting Critias. No one should notice, but be careful not to be seen. You know the little gate in the garden. You also know where my study is – we sat together in there for a while. Do you remember the cedar coffer beside the chair with the high backrest? Bring it home. Understand? You'll be able to carry it.'

'Should I bring the chair, too?' I asked in jest.

'No, of course not, just the box. It contains seven scrolls of my account of the war against the Peloponnesians, up to the summer of nineteenth year, and an eighth scroll from the winter of the nineteenth year up to the summer of the twenty-first year.[143] *The night before you turned up, I fell asleep from exhaustion. The feather slipped from my hand mid-sentence. I wanted to continue working the next morning – there's a mountain of unprocessed material containing information up to the end of the war.*[144] *Please get it to your farm safely. The eighth roll is probably still on the floor, unless Philesia put it back in the box. Keep the documents safe. I know it won't be as easy as it sounds, but I know you can do it. The unprocessed material is in seven boxes – one box for each year.'*

He expected no further questions. He was convinced everything would work as planned and in the end, it did.

He had told me everything I needed to know, with the exception of one small thing. 'Oh, by the way, one more thing. I should really have told you a long while ago: Philesia is my daughter. So now that's out there.' Without waiting for my response, he added: 'I have just one more request: if everything else happens as planned, get Philesia to safety. I still have many friends in the Amphipolis area. You can trust them. They will take her in and protect her.' I was speechless. 'Philesia's mother died in Amphipolis five years ago from a disease even our most talented Greek physicians could not cure. Philesia was only twelve years old. It was terrible. Please take care of her. I trust you to do this.' I nodded without a word.

'Let's go eat,' he said, and turned abruptly from me.

The next morning I leapt onto my horse before the carriage was ready to bring Thucydides to Critias. It was still dark. We had all woken earlier than usual. I arrived in our quarters before dawn to speak with Lysimachus. He didn't return my greeting, saying only: 'There are new orders. Be ready!'

How was I supposed to get the coffers from the house to safety when I had to wait for a mission at the same time? What had the writer been thinking?

We were ready to march for hours, dozing, idle. It was hot. We sweated. The wait was gruelling. Some swore constantly to themselves. Suddenly, Lysimachus burst in.

'The mission is off! Take your horses back to the stables! Give them water – not too much. Give them a rub down, then hit the sack!'

We had already figured that much out. We didn't need to be told, I thought. With a glance at me – did I imagine it? – he added 'Stay in your quarters, understand?' Then he was gone again. Taking care of the horses, removing our armour, stowing the saddles and bridles all took time, but I found an excuse to disappear for a while.

'The feed crates are almost empty,' I called out, 'I'll fetch a few sacks'.

That was a plausible enough excuse. My comrades knew that I had always been dedicated – their words – to the well-being of the horses. Caring for horses was part of my heritage. I was convinced that the horses were our most loyal companions. I can't even begin to count the number of times my horse saved my life, which only made it worse for me that time in Lampsacus: I had to sell my horse to raise the money to get home.[145] With a little help from Zeus Meilichios, our 'benevolent' god, however, I managed to get the horse back. I didn't even have to pay back the 50 Persian darics I had been paid for him![146] Bion and Nausikleides took care of the money – they knew that if I had been forced to sell my horse, then my situation must have been particularly dire. [147] But I digress.

I used the opportunity and hurried to Thucydides' home. The sun was already high in the sky. The coffer with the scrolls was in the study, near the chair. I opened the lid to make sure that they were all still there. Everything was exactly how Thucydides had described it. Even though I should have left the house as quickly as possible, I couldn't resist just reading the last sentence Thucydides had written: 'First, he put in at Ephesus and offered sacrifices to Artemis…' That was the point where he had passed out exhausted, as he had said. Where the feather had slipped from his hand, there was a long, black streak left on the page. The papyrus had fallen to the floor and rolled itself up, as though trying to protect those final words.

I placed the eighth scroll in the coffer, closed the lid, and hid it in a sack I had brought for the purpose. I turned and ran back to our quarters, hid everything in the largest feed crate I could find and emptied a couple of sacks of oats on top of it to fill the crate.

The scrolls would be safe there for a while. In the night, I made for our farm and hid the coffer under my bed. No one saw a thing. Everyone was sleeping peacefully. This could only have been made possible with the grace of god. I felt deep gratitude to the gods in that moment – in the spirit of that strange sophistic lecture that Thucydides had given me. How I was supposed to get the other documents from Thucydides' home, however, was still a complete mystery.

I rode back to Athens under the cover of darkness, collapsing exhausted into my bed in our quarters. No one had noticed my absence.

A Missing Historian

What I didn't know at this point was that Thucydides had not yet returned from his visit to Critias. Had he even reached Critias? I was unsure. Had what I feared would happen actually happened?

When I next set foot in the house, voices were raised. 'Where were you yesterday evening?' demanded Gryllus. Without waiting for my answer, he continued: 'Thucydides hasn't returned. Something must have happened, I know it. Have you heard anything?'

I shook my head and told him about the coffers that were hidden under my bed and said that they should remain hidden. I realised that Gryllus was still waiting for an answer to his question.

'I was here last night,' I replied truthfully, 'but I didn't want to wake anyone. I left before sunrise. You know how tense the situation is!'

'Then you won't have realised what was wrong here. Philesia could hardly stop crying. She just kept sobbing: 'I knew it, I knew it! Why wouldn't he listen to me?' She didn't eat all day. Even old Charicleia couldn't calm her down.'

I was baffled.

'Philesia was asking after you, Xenophon.'

I could hear in my father's voice that he hoped I would be able to calm Philesia. At that moment, she appeared in the doorway, ran up to me, and I took her in my arms.

'Oh Xenophon, Xenophon! Thank the gods you're here!'

The thought that this young woman was the daughter of our guest had occupied my all day, but had also inspired me to carry out my task carefully. Of course, I had never expected to have to fulfil the promise I had made to her father. But now everything was pointing to the fact that my promise would be tested far sooner than expected. It was all too much! I needed Gryllus' help, and wanted to tell him everything. Did Philesia know what her father had made me promise? Did she know that I was to protect her? How could I find that out?

Philesia had already calmed down a bit. 'Should I fetch you something to eat, dear?' asked Charicleia.

'No need, I'll come with you to the kitchen.'

As the two women left for the kitchen, I turned to Gryllus.

'Father, did you know?'

'What do you mean?'

'Thucydides revealed to me last night that Philesia is his daughter.' Gryllus was stunned: 'What? How? That's impossible! Are you telling the truth?'

'Yes, father. I promised Thucydides I would take care of Philesia and make sure she would get home safely to Thrace if something happened to him.'

'Safe? In times like this? It would be best if she stayed here. Besides, I'm sure her father will return soon.'

I didn't see Philesia again that evening. Charicleia took good care of her. Apparently, Philesia went straight to sleep after finally eating.

The Burning House

The next morning, as I rode to Athens, I saw the glow of fire above the city. It was very close to our barracks. I soon realised that it was burning in the vicinity of Thucydides' home. Moments later, I learned the truth: Thucydides' house was ablaze. Charred scraps of papyrus whirled in the morning sky. No one, bizarrely, had tried to extinguish the fire. I was horrified. It was too late. The neighbours seemed unconcerned, having already done enough to ensure the flames would not spread to their houses. Most of them were just watching. Some made bets on when the house would finally collapse.

'What happened? Did someone set it on fire?' someone asked in the staring crowd.

'Minions of the Thirty! No one else!' claimed someone. He didn't seem to be afraid of the fact that these words could get him in serious trouble.

'For sure. There's probably evidence of their crimes in there.'

'What use is this fire to them now? They're on the verge of disappearing anyway. The Tyrant murderers are gathering in Piraeus, they say.'

'Then it was the radical democrats, the Cleonists. They've got plenty to answer for, too. We'll probably never find out who was responsible.'

An old man, standing slightly apart from the main crowd, then raised his voice: 'Last night – or was it the night before? – I saw a sinister character creeping around in the house. I'm always up around that time, and I saw him go through the garden gate. After a little while, he came out with a big sack and disappeared into the darkness.'

I was horrified when I realised what the old man had seen, but he hadn't recognized me. There was no way he could link me with the arsonists.

'Who could it have been? And what was hidden in the sack?' someone asked, excited. 'How should I know? But it was surely whoever set this fire.' 'Nonsense! It's been far too long – why would he not just set the fire immediately rather than wait this long?'

'He didn't set the fire. He just knew that the house was going to be set on fire. He must have come and taken everything of any worth.'

'A looter!'

'Didn't the homeowner notice anything?'

'He must have surprised the intruder and been killed.'

'Was he even in there?'

'Oh!' called out another man, before going on to explain, 'He hasn't been there for days.'

'How do you know?'

'My wife told me. Did you know he lived with a young woman?'

'Really? That old goat?'

'Was she in there?'

'No, of course not. They disappeared together, as far as I know.'

'Someone picked them up in a carriage, my wife says.'

Was it really unreasonable to assume that Critias and his cronies had something to do with this fire? Suddenly, I was making a connection with the disappearance of Thucydides. An absurd thought? Maybe they killed him because they wanted his writings, and he couldn't hand them over because I had taken them to safety. Had he been forced to lead his future murderer to his home to hand over the documents? Had someone, angry when Thucydides couldn't find all of the papers, killed him and burned his house down with him inside?

Was I now responsible for his death too? Would the tragedy not have occurred if I hadn't taken the papers from his house so quickly?

Unthinkable. It would have been easy for the Thirty to take the material from the house and hide it away days ago. No one would have been suspicious if someone had driven up with a cart and taken the scrolls. Things were always being picked up and transported back and forth in Athens.

And if he had not made it to Critias? But no, he was there. The driver had dropped him off at Critias' front door, that much was certain. He just didn't want the carriage to wait for him. He assumed that Critias would take care of his return home. The driver was supposed to set off alone and tell Gryllus that Thucydides had something else to do in the city, and would have to find someone else to take him home later. Was that what really happened? Had the slave told the truth? There was not the slightest bit of evidence that he had left Critias' estate.

'What nonsense!' I said out loud.

'What is?' asked a man who stood beside me, still entranced by the slowly smouldering fire. A handful of people were poking around in the embers to see if anything useful had survived, without success. All that remained were glowing embers and shards of pottery.

'Oh, just thinking out loud,' I replied.

In actuality, the question had shocked me – I felt like I had been discovered. I was afraid that someone might yet recognize me as the intruder. No one was suspicious, however. I shivered, despite my warm riding jacket.

The crowd was beginning to disperse. They were no longer interested in staring at the slowly cooling ashes. An old woman muttered:

'This was a sign from the gods.'

A sign of what, I wondered. I turned away. My horse stood where I had tethered it. That calmed me. I carried no weapons – no one could have guessed that I was one of the Thirty's soldiers, or claim that I had something to do with the fire. My comrades would be waiting for me, I thought, and made to leave the horrible scene as quickly as possible.

If Critias had nothing to do with Thucydides' disappearance and the burning of his home, who did? The Cleonists certainly had a list of fellow citizens they deemed unwelcome. While control of the city was in flux, they could easily take personal revenge on any of their enemies. They lacked only an unscrupulous demagogue such as Cleon, their great idol, who knew how to work the masses into a frenzy. There was always a reason. How would the Spartan occupiers react? Violent clashes would mean spilt blood. On one side there stood the Spartans, with us, the guards of the Thirty; on the other side stood the demos, forever prepared for violence, and long since secretly rearmed. Did Thucydides know something about these events? Was he hidden somewhere in safety? Why then had his home been set ablaze? I saw no connection.

Finally, the uncertain waiting came to an end. We were ordered to patrol outside the city walls – by now barely standing – and report any unusual occurrences to Lysimachus immediately. We were expressly forbidden from getting involved in any violence. Our presence alone should be used to ensure peace and order. It was, in no uncertain terms, not our job to quell an uprising.

Things did not go as expected.

The Liberator

'The rescue came from outside the city. Thrasybulus led a small band of Athenian exiles and emigrants from Boeotia in a surprise attack to seize Phyle in the foothills of Parnitha. After a victory against the Spartan garrison, and after taking Munychia,[148] Thrasybulus had control of Athens' lifeline: Piraeus. Critias and Charmides were killed fighting in the streets, ending the tyranny of the Thirty (end of 404 BC, beginning of 403 BC).'[149]

In Hellenica,[150] Xenophon has a respected man from the organisation committee of the Eleusinian mysteries appear (a 'herald') to call for reconciliation between the warring parties with a powerful speech after the fall of the Thirty. In his speech, he spoke these words to the adherents of the Thirty: 'Obeythe accursed Thirty no longer; they have killed more Athenians in eight months for their own benefit than all the Peloponnesians in ten years of war. Although we might live in peace as fellow citizens, these men have brought about an utterly shameful, terrible, unholy war hated by both gods and men. Rest assured that we, as well as you, have wept bitterly for those slain by our hand.'

With just a few loyal men, the well-respected commander Thrasybulus had managed to occupy Phyle on the border of Athens.[151] With a surprise attack, he took and held the citadel of Munychia in Piraeus with just seventy men.[152] The Spartans were so impressed by Thrasybulus that King Pausanias refrained from taking countermeasures. Finally, he negotiated a ceasefire between the two opposing parties.[153] In the end a general amnesty was declared, and it was thus forgotten who had fought on which side, and what they had done.

This peace, however, was only reached after many deaths.[154] More than seventy men were killed in the carnage. The fallen had their weapons removed, but they were treated with the honour all fallen soldiers were due.

Xenophon's Athenian cavalry was placed under the direct control of the Spartan king. They were ordered to advance in the direction of Piraeus and avoid any contact with the enemy. Numerous skirmishes followed, eventually degenerating into fierce conflict. The Lacedaemonians who marched with Xenophon's division suffered heavy losses, as did the people of Piraeus.

Truce

It was a struggle of man against man. Many knew their opponents. Some fought family, or neighbours with whom they had previously lived peacefully. It was cruel and excruciating.

Finally the gods showed some sympathy. They let the combatants on both sides exhaust themselves to the point that they could scarcely move. That's how it seemed to me, anyway. Most didn't even have the energy to stand, even those who were completely unharmed. Anyone with even a scrap of common sense remaining was willing to end this carnage, but even this lead to a dangerous situation – no one knew whether the enemy was willing to do the same.

Then, however, both sides heard the cry ring out: 'Stop! Stop!' At first, it was just a few voices. Gradually, more joined the chorus, until it was clear that nobody wanted anything else. The fighting let up, and the men just stood in place.

Both sides could see that to continue killing each other was utterly pointless and barbaric. Then everything started to move very quickly. Lysimachus ordered us to our quarters. There, we tended to our wounded as best we could. For our fallen, we prepared an honourable burial in front of the Dipylon Gate leading to the road to Eleusis. We decided against burying their bones in Keramikos, wanting to avoid the usual funeral oration traditional there. Under no circumstances could anything be allowed to jeopardise the peace between the former enemies that had been paid for with so much blood. A funeral oration could arouse unpredictable feelings, and start the violence all over again.

The search for the missing would not be so easily undertaken. The general amnesty also forbade the search for people for the purpose of punishing them. Some expected the missing to simply reappear. Others were afraid the search would just confirm their fears. Yet others were glad that certain citizens had disappeared, never to be seen again. Only the closest of relatives were willing to search for missing family members. Most were not successful.

Eventually, it was left to fate to decide whether the missing would reappear or not. Rumours abounded that some had fled to the Peloponnese, or even to Persia before the flight of the Thirty in order to avoid being held accountable for their crimes. Persia offered unlimited opportunity to begin again. The satraps were delighted to receive immigrants, especially if they came from the Greek polis. The idea that Thucydides was among them could not be denied. Why, though, would he settle in Persia? Why would he disappear without a trace?

The Search for the Missing

Philesia was perhaps the only one who never gave up the search for traces of her father. She would not allow herself to believe he might be dead. I helped her search as best I could. I contacted people who knew him. There weren't many. No know knew anything – we were groping around in the dark. Some still remembered him from before his exile in Thrace. That was no help to us.

I even took to the road for a few weeks to continue the search in Amphipolis and the surrounding area. I was confronted with absurd theories about his murder, but no concrete evidence. Some said he had met a brutal end at the hands of a pair of Thracian brothers. An act of revenge? But why? I discovered he had once imposed a draconian punishment on a thief in one of his goldmines. The man was executed – he was the father of the two alleged killers. Thucydides was said to have tied the thief to a tree and left him there for days without food or water. Unfortunately, the vengeful brothers were nowhere to be found, and no one knew anything about the execution of their father. It was probably just one of countless fanciful tales invented for the pleasure of telling – they even sometimes ended up written down.

The clues led nowhere. Homer could have filled several scrolls with these fantastic stories.

Nevertheless, Philesia convinced me again and again to continue the search. One day, however, it got to be too much. It was almost two years since her father had disappeared, and I snapped: 'It's hopeless! We need a sign from the gods!'

I hadn't been serious, but my words only gave Philesia new hope: 'Why don't we just ask the Oracle at Delphi? The priestess will surely be able to give us an answer.'

With these words, Philesia smiled. She looked at me, full of hope, the way she always did just before I did something she wanted, that I thought was completely pointless

The Oracle at Delphi

An oracle is a person who predicts future events by interpreting evidence left by a higher power, or manifestations of divine will. It can also refer to the site of the oracle. This applied to the 'oracle at Delphi', where Apollo would give a more or less clear answer to the questions of mortals, with the help of a priestess. In Delphi, this was Pythia.[155]

The oracle site in Delphi was a chasm over which the great Temple of Apollo was built. Directly over the chasm there stood a huge tripod holding a metal plate with a hole in it. This was where the priestess sat upon a seat and, intoxicated by the vapours rising from the chasm, made her prophecies. These prophecies were usually ambiguous and obscure, and therefore required interpreting. This was not only an act of worship, but also a lucrative display. Money earned from fees and donations from those who sought answers to their questions flowed in abundance.

Many people worked in the temple, with a variety of roles and tasks. Priests and interpreters of the oracle's prophecies were great minds who were necessary for the operation of the site.

Among the most famous oracles are those who prophesied for the Lydian kings, as recorded by Herodotus. King Gyges, for instance, was confirmed by the oracle at Delphi (Herodotus 1.13). He consequently sent many valuable votive offerings to the temple. One particular admirer of the Delphic oracle was Croesus, who, after careful consideration, visited Delphi over all of the other oracles in Greece and North Africa, convinced that Pythia was the only real oracle (Herodotus 1.48.1). He asked the fateful question of whether or not he should march against the Persians (Herodotus 1.46.3). For safety, he visited not only the Delphic oracle, but also the oracle of Amphiaraus: 'Croesus, king of Lydia and other nations, believing that here are the only true places of divination among men, endows you with such gifts as your wisdom deserves. He asks you now whether he is to send an army against the Persians, and whether he is to add an army of allies'. He asked this question and both oracles gave the same answer. They proclaimed that should Croesus win the war against the Persians, he would destroy a great empire. They also advised him to find the most powerful Greek cities and make alliances with them (Herodotus 1.53)

Croesus was delighted with this answer. He was convinced that he would destroy the kingdom of Cyrus. As always, the oracle, and all of her servants were richly rewarded for this supposed certainty.

Oracle or Secret Police?

'We can try, Philesia, but the oracle's answer depends on how you ask the question. Otherwise, we'll end up getting the same old answers. 'Know thyself!', 'Know that thou art mortal!', 'Moderation in all things!', 'Speak plainly!' and so on.'

Philesia was surprised by my angry remarks. 'You should not make fun of exalted Phoebus Apollo, Xenophon!'

She was on the verge of tears again. I didn't want to hurt her or offend the gods. She just hadn't understood the deeper meaning of my irreverent words. Even the Delphic oracle – I wanted to tell her – couldn't help us now.

But she wouldn't give in: 'Who can we ask for help?' I shrugged and, without really meaning it, responded angrily: 'Let's ask the Persian Great King's secret police, Artaxerxes' bloodhounds, the eyes and ears of the emperor!'[156]

Horrified, she stared at me in disbelief. I had only wanted to make her understand that I thought the search for her father was completely hopeless. Suddenly, however, the idea didn't seem quite so far-fetched. If there was ever anyone who might know something, it was the 'eyes and ears' of the Persian king. It was said they were the best secret police in the world, and they had their agents everywhere.

She had taken me seriously from the start. 'That's one possibility,' she gasped. 'We have to try! But how?' she asked me expectantly.

'No idea, I do not know who might be able to help us.'

Philesia said nothing more. She was sad, and that upset me. In the coming weeks and months, we spoke no more on the matter.

Queen Bee

Philesia was a great help to Charicleia, and was needed everywhere. Everyone loved her. She made sure the house was tidy, took care of our provisions and disciplined the maids and servants. She was exceptionally smart and efficient. She supervised the preparation of our bread and taught the young girls how to use the loom. She made sure that they spent as much time outdoors as possible, and even took care of the farmers' young children. If ever anyone was ill, she knew what to do. In short, she fulfilled all the tasks the gods had imposed on the wife of a landowner.[157]

My father loved her like his own daughter. He compared her – I overheard him saying once – to a queen bee. 'What's that supposed to mean? What about my work makes you think of a queen bee?' she asked, astonished.[158]

'Simple,' replied Gryllus, grinning, 'a queen bee is like a good housewife. She makes sure the bees don't laze around. She leads them and makes them work. She knows exactly what each bee has brought back when she returns from her *flight. She accepts what they bring, and keeps it safe until it's needed. She watches over the construction of the honeycomb, and makes sure her brood is well reared.'*

'Do I have to stay in the house like a queen bee, then, while the others work in the field?'

'Exactly. You send people out there that need to do their jobs, to work, everyone in their proper place, and watch over the others who have their duties in the house. You make sure the harvested fruits are properly processed, organise the provisions and make sure that they're not used up after just a few weeks and that nothing is wasted. You make sure that the clothes we need are made from the wool of the sheep...'

'All of that would surely not be possible,' Philesia interjected, 'if the people didn't work diligently in the fields and stables.'

'Ah yes, but all their work would be pointless if there were no one to properly process and carefully store the harvest,' countered Gryllus with a smile. He was thinking of my mother, Diodora. He was silent for a moment, a smile still on his lips, before he continued in a firm voice: 'It may seem like difficult, arduous work to you, dear Philesia, but there are activities here that can bring people a lot of joy, too. Just the other day, Charicleia was telling me how proud she felt watching you teach the young girls to use the loom and how to bake good bread, or telling stories and singing songs to the children.'

I had the impression that these words were not solely directed at Philesia. They were also meant for me. Charicleia seemed to see it that way too, and was looking at me with a knowing smile.

'Why are you smiling like that?' I asked her.

'Don't you understand why your father said these things to Philesia where you could hear them?'

Her words confused me for a moment. 'I don't know what you mean, Charicleia' I asked, but without waiting for her reply, I left quickly, calling back only 'I have to go, I'm going to be late.'

Old Lykus was waiting with my saddled horse. He helped me onto the horse. On the way to Athens, I considered the conversation between Gryllus and Philesia and Charicleia's words. Certainly, I was fond of Philesia. She was not only capable, but very beautiful too. There was no doubt about that. But Thucydides had entrusted her to me – so to speak – and I had promised to protect and care for her. Since then, there had been an invisible wall between us. This did not, however, conceal my mood from Philesia.

'What's wrong, Xenophon?' she asked me once. 'Have I done something? Why are you so quiet? Say something! I don't understand.'

My answer was meaningless: 'It's nothing. You're imagining things' I avoided her as best I could. I did not want to betray her father's trust.

I helped in her search for Thucydides only half-heartedly. Then one day she remembered the 'eyes and ears' of the Great King: 'You wanted to ask them...'

In reality I wanted nothing of the sort. Not long after, however, I suddenly received a letter from my friend Proxenus in Thebes.[159] *It was late autumn in the year Xenainetos held the office of Archon, and about a year before Socrates died.*[160]

The Letter

Diogenes Laërtius (around 250 AD) writes in his work *Lives and Opinions of Eminent Philosophers* (2.49 f): 'Xenophon gained the friendship of Cyrus in the following way: he had an intimate friend named Proxenus, a Boeotian, a pupil of Gorgias of Leontini and a friend of Cyrus. Proxenus, while living in Sardis at the court of Cyrus, wrote a letter to Xenophon at Athens, inviting him to come and seek the friendship of Cyrus. Xenophon showed this letter to Socrates and asked his advice. Socrates sent him to Delphi to ask the gods for advice. Xenophon complied and came into the presence of the god. He inquired, not whether he should go and seek service with Cyrus, but in what way he should do so. For this Socrates blamed him, yet at the same time he advised him to go. On his arrival at the court of Cyrus he became as warmly attached to him as Proxenus himself. We have his own sufficient narrative of all that happened on the expedition and on the return home (in his book *Anabasis*).'

In Xenophon's words: 'In the army (of Cyrus) there was a certain Xenophon of Athens. He was neither general nor captain nor private, but had accompanied the expedition because Proxenus, an old friend of his, had brought him from his home and promised that, if he came along, he would become friends with Cyrus.'[161]

Proxenus was very ambitious. From childhood, he was to accomplish great deeds through sheer strength of will. This led him to become a student of the sophist Gorgias, whom he paid a vast fee to teach him. In order to be able to exert power, he sought to become close to powerful people. For this reason, he got himself involved in the as-yet unknown plans of the Persian prince, in whose service he hoped to make a name for himself and to earn a fortune. He never once, however, tried to reach his goals dishonestly. Rather, he was convinced that a man should follow his intentions in a respectable and honest fashion. Whether or not he had the disposition of a leader is questionable.[162] He was not particularly assertive, and his soldiers regularly gave him the run around.

The fact that Xenophon spoke with Socrates about the contents of the letter, he explains with the political brilliance of trip to Persia. He could, Socrates feared, invite blame from the city of Athens through his proximity to Cyrus – it was well known that the Persian prince had actively supported the Lacedaemonians in the final phase of the Peloponnesian war.[163]

Socrates' concern that Xenophon would get into trouble so soon after the war if he were to come into contact with a prominent Persian – the brother of the Great King, no less – was certainly not unfounded. His decision to go to Persia was should not, however, have been critical to his later sentencing to exile.

The Decision

'Philesia,' I called out, excited, 'I have news!'

I ran to her with the letter in my hand. She thought I had finally found a trace of her father. All I could tell her, however, was what Proxenus had offered me. Somewhat awkwardly, I explained to her: 'I met him during my studies in Athens. Since then, we've been each other's guest – that is to say, he had a place for me to stay when I was in Thebes and he stays with me when he's here. He writes that I should visit him in Sardis. He wants to introduce me to Cyrus, the brother of the Great King, so we can get to know each other.'

'That's wonderful! That means you can…'

'Exactly, I will be able… if everything goes well, I will be able to find news of your father with Cyrus' help.'

'Can I come with you?' asked Philesia, elated.

'Why not? But we must think carefully.'

I avoided a clearer answer. In reality, I had no intention of bringing her to Persia. I was expecting an exciting and possibly even dangerous journey, setting off from Piraeus, before travelling by ship for the next several days to Ephesus, and then by land for around three days until we reached Sardis.[164] I wanted to be able to travel freely, and not be responsible for anyone else along the way – and certainly not Philesia. If I were to bring her with me, I thought, she would expect me to spend the entire time in Sardis searching for traces of her father. Of course, I intended to do that, but not just that.

The Persian prince should be a fascinating person. Proxenus spoke about him with such passion that I wanted to meet him immediately, and spend as much time with him as possible, as I let Philesia know.

'I understand that,' she replied, coolly. She suspected that Cyrus was more important to me at that moment than she and her father were. She didn't even want me to continue reading out the letter.

'What's wrong, Philesia?'

'For a long time, I've felt like you're not interested in this task, in our task. Sometimes I even think you just don't care about anything. When the Thirty Tyrants disappeared, I think your affection for me went with them.'

She was deeply disappointed. The fact that she felt as though my feelings for her had disappeared with the fall of the Thirty irritated me somewhat. That had nothing to do with anything! Of course, the power struggle in Athens had not left me unaffected. The leadership was different, and we were no longer needed. Our duties had been reduced to caring for the horses. The general amnesty had at least allowed for one practically painless fresh start. At least, that was how I saw it.

'What does the change of government in Athens have to do with our feelings for each other?' I asked her.

'If only you could have seen your face when I said I wanted to go with you to Sardis...!'

She had seen through me. What she suspected was true. To be honest, Thucydides no longer interested me at that point. Without meaning to, Proxenus had made me want to leave everything that had been important to me behind. Philesia, Thucydides, the scrolls in their hiding place under my bed, Gryllus, Charicleia.

That night, I was too excited to sleep. Every time I closed my eyes, I saw Sardis, Cyrus, Proxenus, Persia. Then the worry would return. My father would hopefully understand if I left him alone for a few weeks or months. He had Philesia to help him around the house, and Charicleia. The two women had everything under control. But what impression would it give if I, a member of the Athenian cavalry, went searching for the friendship of a Persian satrap? There had never been real peace between Athens and the Persian empire. Persia had contributed significantly to the Athenian disaster in the last war. Without the vast financial resources of the Persians, Sparta would not have emerged victorious.

I am not exaggerating when I say that there were plenty of advocates for democracy in Athens who were just waiting for an opportunity to pin something on 'sympathisers' with the Thirty, as they called me and my colleagues, or to at least be rid of us since they could not drag us into a courtroom due to the amnesty. In Sardis, I would no longer have to face the dark and reproachful eyes of my fellow Athenian citizens. It was unbearable, and meant I only went out if I absolutely had to. Because no one had any use for us after the coup, many of us had joined the Spartan or Persian services. It was comforting that we were welcome there. It was also the reason why we were unceremoniously declared traitors.

So to the democrats it was just more fuel for the flames when I went to Sardis. I was accused of letting down not only my father and our farm, but even my own homeland, because I was dealing with the enemy.

Ultimately, I could even end up being sentenced to lifelong exile in absentia – a possibility I didn't really take seriously at the beginning of my adventure in Persia. There was enough evidence for my love of Persia. One only had to pay the miserable sycophants[165] enough, and suddenly I was a traitor.

The reasons for and against my Persian adventure were in perfect balance, it seemed to me. Philesia and my father did not decline. The decision weighed on me. I couldn't make Proxenus wait any longer. In Athens, I found my honoured teacher Socrates in the market. He was, as ever, surrounded by young men. When he saw me, he immediately approached: 'Who do we have here? Xenophon, my dear Xenophon! How lovely it is to see you again at last. How is farming, horse breeding and hunting with the dogs treating you? And let's not forget the art of riding!'

Xenophon's 'Short Writings'

When Socrates asked this question, Xenophon had indeed mentioned these interests, but he had not yet written anything on these topics. His 'short writings' did not appear until between 390 BC and 355 BC.

In *Oeconomicus* (after 390 BC), Xenophon reproduces a Socratic dialogue about household management and agriculture. It contains advice on managing a farm. It first concerns itself with the duties of a housewife, in particular a housewife's responsibility for keeping the house tidy and distributing work skilfully. The duties of the master of the house include, among other things, jurisdiction over the slaves and the selection of suitable employees. Subsequently, the dialogue concentrates on specific agricultural issues. Xenophon describes the leadership of the master of the house in more detail, which does not differ significantly from a general's leadership. The connection between agricultural and military proficiency is Xenophon's educational ideal.

Hipparchicus, (written after 362 BC) outlines the duties of a cavalry officer. It is less a systematic treatise and more a set of rules for a practitioner, including selection of a horse and rider for combat, deployment of troops, tactical directions, stratagems, treatment of soldiers, defence of a city, suggestions for expanding the Athenian cavalry and comments on the necessity of upholding cult regulations.

The companion for cavalry men *On Horsemanship* (written around 360 BC) deals with the purchase of horses and horse equipment, including the condition of the stalls, horse care and training for military horses. The author discusses topics including running and jumping training, uphill and downhill riding and combat techniques. The writing demonstrates great expertise and animal psychology skills.

In *Ways and Means* (written after 355 BC), Xenophon considers how Athens can ensure its economic power in spite of its abandonment of expansionist policies. He describes Athens' resources, points out the usefulness of metics (resident aliens), and makes suggestions for the elimination of discrimination against them. He explains his ideas for the expansion of shipping and trade, the intensification of the promotion of silver and the strengthening of investment policies during prosperous times. This piece is early evidence of the development of economic thinking in politics.

A Short Trip to Delphi

Socrates alluding to my interests was not very flattering. He didn't take these activities particularly seriously. He made fun of physical labour and technical ability every chance he got. That offended me all the more because he also never missed an opportunity to pour scorn on my 'body cult', as he called it. The only person who ever seemed to be on my side, unfortunately, was Antisthenes, who could be quite contentious. The distinguished and extremely arrogant Plato also couldn't stand me, but he was not there at the time. Of course, Socrates protected me, but probably only because he disliked the behaviour of wealthy young men, not because of any inner conviction.

He added 'Our Xenophon doesn't just know about guiding ploughs and taming horses; he's also a devoted admirer of Hercules! You might even say he's the next Hercules, choosing a life of toil and hard work. You all know wise Prodicus' story about the young Hercules at the crossroads? A superb story!'[166] This time there were no taunts from my 'classmates'. No one laughed. Dirty looks were thrown in my direction. Was it jealousy because Socrates had been so obviously pleased to see me?

He placed his hand on my left shoulder and said, quietly 'Walk with me a while!' I immediately mentioned the letter from my friend Proxenus. Socrates was unsurprised. 'I've heard stories about the young prince's charms. I, too, would like the opportunity to meet and talk with him. You know I don't enjoy travelling, though. Only when I have to fulfil my duty as a hoplite.' He laughed, but then became very serious. 'Can't you imagine the offence it would cause in Athens if you travelled to Persia to become Cyrus' friend? You do know that the Persians aided the Lacedaemonians in the war, don't you?'

'Yes, I know, but I'm not plotting against my home city. That would be idiotic. I'm fascinated by the Persians – I'm taking the opportunity to learn about a new world.'

'I understand that, Xenophon, but I strongly advise you to go to Delphi and ask the gods about your plans. I hope with all my heart that everything goes well for you.'

Socrates turned away quickly. I watched him until he vanished in the crowd.

Back home, I declared my intentions. I wanted to depart for Delphi immediately and get the advice of the gods. My father only murmured: 'Hopefully they'll advise you to stay at home!' Philesia remained silent. She wanted nothing more than the permission of the oracle for her own reasons.

The next morning I rode alone, but with two horses, to the northwest. Delphi was located in Phocis, at the foot of the Phaedriades of Parnassus. The sacred way led to the Temple of Apollo. I had formulated my question in writing, as was tradition: 'To which god should I offer sacrifice in order to gain their support? To which god should I pray for my upcoming trip to Persia to go well and that I come back safe?'

I sought out a priest and handed him the rolled and sealed sheet on which I had written my question. I also gave him the customary donation. Fortunately, I had arrived at a good time for the temple. It took only two days for me to receive my answer from the gods. I then took the prescribed sacrificial actions. Suppliants drew lots to determine order – I was lucky, as I ended up near the front of the queue. The priest told me – in writing, too – the name of the god to whom I had to pray. It was Zeus Basileus, the protector of the polis.

Once I returned to Athens, I immediately went to Socrates to tell him what I had learned from the oracle. The philosopher was visibly upset that I had not simply asked whether or not I should go on the journey at all. 'You must do what the gods have commanded, since you asked the way you did.'[167]

I was sorry that I had displeased the admired master, but there was nothing to be done about it now. I carried out my sacrifice for Zeus Basileus as directed.

I would later include this episode in Anabasis for a specific reason – I wanted to avoid the possibility that someone could blame Socrates for my decision. No one should ever be able to claim that Socrates had made me a friend of the Persians and the Spartans![168]

Farewell

Gryllus actually accompanied me to the port. Even Philesia wanted to watch as I boarded the ship. I had only a little luggage, but I rented a carrier. He placed my things in the covered stern of the sailing ship to which the captain had directed him. A huge number of amphorae - possibly as many as 2,000 - were tied down with ropes in the belly of the ship. They stood in stable wooden frames so they *wouldn't tip over even without the ropes. Presumably they contained olive oil or wine.*

I said goodbye quickly to my father and to Philesia. Neither of them said a word. She had tears in her eyes. Gryllus embraced me silently, as he always did when I left for a long time. Philesia grabbed my right hand. She gave me a fleeting kiss on the cheek. I breathed in the scent of her hair. I could feel her sadness. It practically broke my heart.

'Oh Philesia!' I didn't need to say anything more. I didn't want her to see how moved I was.

On Board

There were other passengers boarding besides me. Most were wrapped in long coats. There were dark figures among them. Were they perhaps Persian agents? Everyone was given a thick reed mat and told to look for a place to sleep. It wasn't particularly difficult to find somewhere. I quickly found a spot a respectful distance from the putative agents of the Persian Great King.

Two men were actually speaking to each other in Persian. My knowledge of the language at that time was not particularly strong. I understood only a few unconnected words. The two Persians had probably been in Attica on business for a few weeks. They seemed pleased with the success of their business. I thought I could make out a few names: Lysander, Critias, Thrasybulus… they were probably discussing the exciting events of the past few weeks. Perhaps they had even been in Athens to gauge the political situation and were now returning to Susa, where they would report to their superiors about the events.

The ship didn't set off until late afternoon. Philesia and Gryllus had surely long since returned home. I hadn't wanted them to wait until the ship launched. It was cool. I wrapped my travelling cloak around myself and pulled my petasos down over my face. The wide brim protected me against the increasingly strong westerly winds.

In the night, it began to rain, but I slept deeply and dreamlessly. I woke to a warm spring sun.[169] *I ate a piece of barley bread, packed for me in a travelling pack by Charicleia. The Persians had probably been awake for a while already. They chewed listlessly on pieces of dried meat and drank something from a leather skin. I watched them discreetly out of the corner of my eye. They didn't seem to have noticed me, but I couldn't be certain. Could they possibly belong to the 'eyes and ears' of the Great King? Should I address them? They clearly understood Greek, otherwise they wouldn't have been sent to Athens – for any reason whatsoever.*

It took me a whole day to approach my fellow travellers. It was not as easy as it sounds. As I crept between the amphorae towards them, they regarded me with amusement. 'Hail, strange man from Athens!' I was happily surprised to hear my mother tongue.

'Hail, men from mighty Persia!' Embarrassed, I asked the obvious question: 'Are you going to Ephesus?'

'Indeed. Whether we arrive safely, however, only the gods know.' The ice was broken. The apparently sinister wayfarers were friendly people. They were obviously happy to have some variety on the otherwise monotonous sea voyage. The long daggers they wore under their cloaks, however, gave me pause. My own scimitar probably worried them, too, however, no matter how hard I tried to hide it from their sight, but I wasn't about to go without adequate protection when travelling. A sword or a dagger startled robbers and highwaymen far more reliably than a simple walking stick.

'Do you live in Ephesus, or are you just stopping on your way?' Was this an interrogation? Had they realised that I regarded them as agents of the Great King? 'This isn't an interrogation' said the younger man suddenly, much to my surprise. 'We're no secret agents!'

I was speechless. Were they mind readers? Of course not. I tried to turn the tables on them and get them to reveal more about themselves. 'I am Xenophon, son of Gryllus.'

'My name is Autoboisakes,' the elder of the two replied in a friendly voice, 'I come from Troas, specifically Dardanos, on the Hellespont. We are explorers for our mighty Great King. We do nothing more than your famous Herodotus of Halicarnassus.'

The younger man added: 'I am Bagaios of Ephesus.'

Herodotus of Halicarnassus.

Herodotus of Halicarnassus lived from 484 BC to around 430 BC. He came from a well-known Carian-Greek family and participated in the domestic political struggles in his homeland. He was, for example, involved in a conspiracy against the tyrant Lygdamis, was exiled and lived on the island of Samos for a long time. He later returned and helped to ensure that the tyrant could never seize power again. Subsequently he went to Athens, where he was connected with Pericles and the famous tragedian Sophocles, with whom he was close friends.

Herodotus wrote a major work of history in nine books. He opens his narrative work with the following announcement: 'Here is displayed the inquiry of Herodotus of Halicarnassus, so that the deeds of man not be lost to time, and that great and marvellous deeds, some displayed by the Greeks, some by the barbarians, not be forgotten.'

In largely imaginary verbal and indirect speeches within the context of the ongoing story, Herodotus illustrates what he perceives to be the driving forces of history. He has, for example, the Greek commander Themistocles before the Battle of Salamis in 480 BC say (8.60): 'Men usually succeed when they have reasonable plans. If their plans are unreasonable, the god does not wish to assent to human intentions.' Here, the realisation of mortal intentions is made dependant on the approval of the gods: they guide events and support reasonable plans, otherwise, they rule over the world according to unknowable laws.

Herodotus' objective was not to thoroughly investigate historical facts and record them chronologically. He wanted to explain the course of history in an appealing manner and make its meaning make sense. He frequently had to admit that the 'truth' of his information could not be proven. In the novel-like parts of his book, he also tried to make his findings on the legitimacy of historical practice vivid: the gods seemed to ensure poetic justice, but were ultimately unpredictable.

In spite of all the specialities and achievements of foreign peoples, Herodotus remains convinced that the historic merit of being the 'saviour of Greece' in the conflict between the Greeks and the Persians belonged to Athens alone (7.139), because the majority of Greeks were not prepared to fight for freedom from bondage and in fact remained friendly to Persia.

An example of Herodotus' reporting is his telling of the events that led to the death of Leonidas and the 300 Spartans (*Histories* 7.201–233). First, he describes the military situation. Under the leadership of Leonidas, the Greeks have taken their position in the pass of Thermopylae. Xerxes was north of the pass, while the area south was still under Greek control. With evidence that the attacker is no god, but a man who will one day fall from power, the Greeks won more allies. Leonidas approached Thermopylae with 300 men 'all of whom had sons'. According to Herodotus, this was done for its psychological effect: the Spartans allow Leonidas to take this position so that the other allies will follow his example and yield to the Persian king without a fight. However, Xerxes' continued advance causes the majority of the Greek troops to retreat to build a defensive line further south. Leonidas decides he will not relinquish his position, even though he knows he is not in a positions to resist the Persian attack with his men. The Persian king does not understand what he views as the absurd behaviour of the Spartans.

Damaratus, the former Spartan king, who had been deposed for his friendly attitude towards Persia and who had found asylum in the Persian court, tells him bluntly:

'These men are coming to fight us for the pass, and they are preparing. That is their custom: When they are about to risk their lives, they decorate their heads. Know, however, that if you overcome these men and those remaining behind at Sparta, there is no one else on earth who will withstand you. You are now attacking the fairest kingdom in Hellas and the bravest men.'

The Persian king reacts with confusion – in his eyes the patience of the Spartans is a sign of stupidity and effrontery.

Cicero (*De legibus* 1.5) later called Herodotus the 'father of Greek history'. In fact, Herodotus was a decisive impetus. Not only did he find a literary form which combined the instruction and entertainment of the listener, but he also formulated the basic motive behind all future historiography: the preservation of the memory of human events. Thucydides explicitly associated himself with Herodotus,[170] but distances himself from him in his Methods chapter (1.22) without mentioning him by name. He expressly renounces telling – as Herodotus did – 'nice stories'. He wanted, on the contrary, to deliver cold, hard facts. This resulted in Herodotus gaining a reputation for being a less-than-serious historian, and he was only taken seriously in the fields of ethnography and paradoxography, the art of telling fantastic stories.

Today, Herodotus is seen as an inquisitive teacher and journalist who gathered his information through autopsy, local stories and interviews with natives and enriched it with his own ideas, judgements and religious beliefs. From a completely unglamorous place, his account of Egypt (2.99.1), he describes his work as a journalist: 'So far, all I have said is the record of my own autopsy and judgement and inquiry. Henceforth I will record Egyptian chronicles, according to what I have heard, adding something of what I myself have seen.'

Obviously he was aware of the fact that by adding information he couldn't prove himself, he brought an element of uncertainty into his work. Nevertheless, he explained explicitly (7.152,2) that 'I am obliged to report the news; I am not, however, obliged to believe it, and this view should apply for my entire account.'

What do the Persians Know about Thucydides?

'Have you met Herodotus?' I asked my Persian travelling companions excitedly, even though I knew he had died over thirty years ago.

'When Herodotus died in the Greek colony of Thurii in southern Italy, I had not yet been born. Autoboisakes however...' Turning to his companion, he continued: 'You should answer the question.'

'The story teller,' said the older man, 'was a well-travelled man. He knew the entire world – Asia, Egypt, Greece, and the battlegrounds of our great war, the land of Scythians, the Black Sea, Thrace, our Persian empire... he gave lectures about his travels in Athens. I had the chance to hear one. I was only fifteen at the time. I was allowed to accompany my father Tigranes to Greece. He was commissioned by our former Great King Artaxerxes Macrocheir,[171] the grandfather of our current Great King Artaxerxes Mnemon[172] to undertake a diplomatic mission.'

I listened in stunned silence. Of course, I didn't know at the time that his younger brother wanted to remove Cyrus from the throne.

'I am now 60 years old,' the Persian continued 'and I have never since met a man as wise as your Herodotus, Greek or Persian, although...'

Impatiently, I interrupted the son of Tigranes. 'Autoboisakes, if you met Herodotus, Pericles and Sophocles, then surely you must have encountered our historian Thucydides at least once?'

'Oh, a shame!' Bagaios interjected. 'You're opening deep wounds now!'

'Leave it, Bagaios', said Autoboisakes with a soothing smile, 'I am happy to answer Xenophon's question: When I think of Thucydides, I feel only sadness and pain.'

'What do you know of him? Is he dead?' I spluttered, dismayed.

'Oh no, no' said the Persian. 'I am overcome with sadness when I think of what his home city did to him, the twenty years of exile, and then the endangerment of his life by the radical democrats. He had nothing to do with the regime of the Thirty. They allowed him to return from Thrace only so that he could complete his work about your great war in Athens.' Finally, he came back to my question: 'Yes, I met him, when I visited Athens for the first time almost 40 years ago. He is somewhat older than I. Before the war, we met again more or less coincidentally. He was a guest of the politician Antiphon of Rhamnus, of whom he was very fond.[173] I had heard of his difficult, but fortunate recovery from illness. You Greeks have excellent doctors.'[174]

'Did you hear about the affair with Amphipolis?'

'Of course! He was not responsible for that failed undertaking, though. Hence why we in Persia didn't understand why he was exiled from Athens after the conquest of Amphipolis by the legendary Lacedaemonian Brasidas.'

'Why else would he have been exiled?'

'I still believe the Athenians simply wanted to get rid of him. He asked too many question and analysed the war so thoroughly right from the start that the Athenians were afraid of the truth. We call him 'the enlightener'. That was certainly his official title in the court of our Great King.'

'Is it true that he spent a lot of time in Persia while he was away from Athens?' I asked curiously.

'Yes, his investigations led him to us, as well.' He wanted to know every reason behind the events – every cause and every effect. He must have written so many documents and papers back in Thrace! Our Great King always supported him. I myself was ordered to provide him with information about everything I could. He always told me he was happy and making good progress with his work.'

Suddenly, he fell silent. I wanted to hear more. 'When did you see him last?'

'I met him in Athens two years ago. The Thirty were already in power. I was negotiating the future of Greek cities on our western coast again for our Great King. I naturally asked him for his opinion, and about the state of his work. He said he only needed a few more weeks. He had all his material together.'

Even though he wasn't an agent, Autoboisakes, as a long-time diplomat, had a wealth of information at his disposal about the secret service. That was obvious. But did the Persians know more than this friendly diplomat?

Bagaios seemed to have recognized my unspoken question: 'The eyes and ears of the Great King know nothing more about Thucydides. But not to worry – there's no reason not to believe he is still alive.'

Arrival in Ephesus

Eventually, the conversation returned to general trivialities. The journey was difficult, but not unpleasant. The weak westerly wind drove us slowly and without incident to Ephesus in less than four days. My Persian companions bade me farewell and climbed aboard a waiting carriage. Earlier, they had formally invited me to visit them in Persepolis when I next had the chance. I thanked them sincerely, but I couldn't ever imagine visiting at that time.

The Persians' carriage had hardly departed when a short burly man with dark skin stepped up to me and asked, in Greek: 'Sir, are you Xenophon of Athens?' I nodded, somewhat surprised. Immediately, he responded: 'I was sent by the Theban general Proxenus. I am to accompany you to Sardis.' He had already been waiting for three days. He asked after me on every ship from Piraeus.

I was surprised. 'Every ship? How many was that?'

'Oh, well, just two in three days,' he replied meekly. He obviously felt he had been caught out exaggerating. I let the issue drop, and asked him his name.

'I am Xanthus, the blonde. At least that's what Proxenus calls me.' He grinned broadly at that. His large, round head was shaved bald. The stubble that was visible was pitch-black.

Xanthus had rented a room for me in a large pandocheion where I could spend the night. The next morning I was to travel to Sardis. The trip would take a couple of days. 'Everything you need is taken care of,' he said confidently.

'Where are you staying?' I asked Xanthus.

'Don't worry about me, sir. I know a flute player. She'll happily take me in for an octobol. A lovely girl – she plays the flute beautifully,' he said, smirking.

'Good luck, Xanthus!'

'Thank you, sir.' Xanthus accompanied me to the hostel before hurrying away.

The house was overcrowded. It was dark and awfully loud. My bedroom had no door, just a light, tattered curtain separating my night quarters from the taproom. I heard people screaming chaotically. They were constantly screaming the same words: 'Girl, I'm parched, bring me another tankard! And don't be like that!' Sometimes, I could hear the soft, dulcet tones of a flute from somewhere in the distance. I thought about Xanthus and his bedfellow, the girl for an octobol.

Just before I fell asleep, I heard a man call out: 'Let's drag the storyteller out of bed! He can tell us about the beautiful widow – we are in Ephesus, aren't we?'

'Is her dead husband still hanging on the cross?' I heard someone else say.

'What? A dead man on a cross?'

'Yes! She saved the life of her lover with the body of her husband.'

'How did she do that?'

'She sat in the sepulchre sobbing and wishing she were as dead as her husband. The watchman guarding the crosses of the recently executed heard her. He went to the sepulchre and tried to comfort her.'

'Comfort her? How?'

'Simple, she was starved half to death. He brought her something to eat. At first, she didn't want to touch a thing. Eventually, she took a few bites, and her spirit began to return. And then he comforted her himself.'

'What do you mean?'

'Man, are you stupid? How else would you comfort a young, beautiful widow?'

Everyone burst into laughter.

'But the worst is still to come.'

'What happened? Did she die anyway?'

'No! But the little adventure almost cost her lover his life!'

Everyone laughed again, but this time it sounded gleeful.

'No, I said "almost". While he was distracted, one of the bodies disappeared from one of the crosses.'

'How?'

'Simple, some of his relatives fetched him down. The watchman was busy in the tomb with the widow. After a little while, though, he returned to the cross to find it as naked as the widow he had just been "comforting".'

'What happened then?' We were all waiting for the answer.

'The couple in love dragged the dead husband out of his sarcophagus, stripped him naked and bound him to the cross as a replacement for the man who had disappeared. But you know that already.'

'That really happened here in Ephesus?'

Finally, everyone was satisfied, and no one needed to wake the storyteller.[175]

Onwards to Sardis

The next day, we set off for Sardis. Xanthus had taken care of everything. In a crowded carriage, the trip took three days. The travellers hardly spoke to each other the entire time. Most slept. The horses had to rest often, as the road was littered with stones. In some places, our progress was even impeded by huge boulders. From time to time, we stopped to water the horses. The driver and his assistant unhitched them and led them to a pond or stream. It gave us the chance to stretch our legs. Winter was not yet over and you could feel the cold. The grey, hard-packed snow reminded me of the years when you could get here only by foot or by horse and cart.

At night, we travellers slept in shabby tents. Most of the time it was snowing or raining. Luckily, I had my coat and my big hat.

On the last day of our journey, I witnessed a sign from god.[176] *Not far from the road, I saw a fierce screaming eagle perched on a stone. Coincidentally, there was a seer among the other travellers. For him, the event was an important sign. The eagle was, after all, the bird of Zeus. This suggested that it wasn't simply an everyday happening, but something more. The eagle promised – according to the seer – fame, but also a tremendous struggle, since the eagle had been struggling to ward off a flock of crows. The signs promised fame and glory, but no material profit, because the bird of prey only caught its prey in flight.*

What did Zeus want to say to me with this sign? I would only be able to get a convincing answer if I could find a sacrificial animal to slaughter. Obviously, that option wasn't available to me. The only thing I could do was contemplate and hope that I would be able to overcome the difficulties. I wasn't that interested in material gain anyway.

Later, it would become apparent that the gods, as they had from the beginning, were still helping me through their signs to make the right decision.

The Ancient Capital

Sardis was the old capital of the kingdom of Lydia. The fabulously wealthy and powerful Croesus once ruled there. Cyrus the Great, founder of the Persian empire, conquered Lydia, as Herodotus plausibly explains[177]:

'The Persians conquered Sardis and took Croesus prisoner. Croesus had ruled fourteen years and been besieged fourteen days. Fulfilling the oracle's prophecy, he had destroyed a great empire – his own. The Persians took him and brought him to Cyrus. Cyrus erected a pyre and mounted Croesus atop it, bound in chains, with twice seven sons of the Lydians beside him. Cyrus may have intended to sacrifice him as a victory-offering to some god, or he may have wished to fulfil a vow, or perhaps he had heard that Croesus was a pious man and wanted to find out if some divinity would deliver him from being burned alive. So Cyrus did this. As Croesus stood on the pyre, even though he was in such a wretched position, Solon's words, granted to him by a god, occurred to him: No man among the living is fortunate. When this occurred to him, he heaved a deep sigh and, after long silence, he called out Solon's name three times. Cyrus heard and ordered the interpreters to ask Croesus who he was invoking. Croesus explained how the Athenian Solon had once visited him and been unimpressed by his wealth; he had contempt not only for him, but for all people who thought themselves fortunate. Now everything had turned out for Croesus as Solon had said. Cyrus reflected on this, and that he was also such a person.'

Cyrus wanted to bring the unfortunate man down from the stake. But the fire burnt on. He begged Apollo for help. Apollo, to extinguish the fires, brought a powerful downpour. In the future, Cyrus became a wise counsellor for Croesus.

Reunion with Proxenus

In Sardis, Xanthus led me to a large, walled park. I was astounded. There were many tents on the side of the path leading to a stately palace. Men sat in front of the tents cleaning the weapons, patching clothes and shoes, preparing food and talking loudly with each other. I thought I could even hear words in my own language. There was a diverse mix of people from all over the world.

Xanthus noticed my astonishment. 'Don't you know what's going on here?' he asked me, incredulous.

'No, Proxenus wants to introduce me to the Persian prince, that's all I heard. I also hope he will be able to help me in my search for a missing Athenian. The Persian secret police are famous for having information on everything under the sun. Take me to Proxenus!'

'Yes sir, I'll take you to his tent.'

Proxenus was sitting in front of a large tent, from which could be heard a murmur of voices. I couldn't understand a word, but I could sense a lot of excitement. Xanthus announced me to a guard who stood before the entrance. Proxenus appeared immediately. He was visibly happy to see me. Of course, first he asked how me and my father were, and how my journey from Piraeus across the sea to Ephesus, and from Ephesus to Sardis had been.

'I'll announce us to Cyrus immediately. He's excited to see you! I just need to send the men in my tent away – we've spoken enough already.

He said goodbye to the men, whom I recognized as Greeks. They were Theban officers.

In the Residence of the Persian Prince

Proxenus and I finally entered the palace of the Persian prince. Xanthus ran ahead to announce us. We sat on a bench and waited. After some time, a double door opened, and the younger brother of the Great King appeared. He was not wearing the lavish robes I knew the Persians wore to receive foreigners or supplicants. He said only: 'Greetings, men of Hellas. I am pleased to meet you, and bid you welcome to our holy city of Sardis. So this is your friend from Athens, the noble Xenophon.'

'Yes, Cyrus, he has just arrived. He would like to greet you,' replied Proxenus. 'Xenophon is not only an excellent rider, he is also an accomplished horse breeder. His father Gryllus' stud farm is known even in Persia. He could be an excellent consultant for us on all matters concerning the cavalry.'

'Always happy,' said Cyrus, fixing me with stare, 'to meet an expert in such an important field. You would certainly be a valuable advisor and consultant. We're marching against the Pisidians tomorrow.[178] *They have settlements south-east of here, and they refuse to obey the Great King, regrettably. To this end, I have gathered Greek soldiers and their leaders here.'*

I was very surprised. For the simple punishment of disobedient subjects of the Great King, the forces that Cyrus had gathered and was continuing to gather were hugely disproportionate. Even the weapons seemed inappropriate to me. Everything seemed to indicate a large campaign.

I couldn't imagine that Cyrus had recruited an expensive army of Greek mercenaries only to use it against an admittedly rapacious, but otherwise insignificant hill tribe. Obviously, I kept quiet – I wasn't here as a general, nor as a captain, or a lowly soldier.[179]

I trusted Cyrus, because – it was said – Persians learn three things from childhood: horseback riding, archery, and telling the truth. So said Herodotus.[180]

Cyrus

Cyrus, the younger brother of the Persian Great King Artaxerxes, lived from 423 BC to 401 BC. In Anabasis (1.9.9–28), Xenophon paints a portrait of the prince, whom he believes to be the ideal king, with excellent sovereign virtues.[181] Proxenus introduced him to the prince,[182] but it is difficult to imagine that this led to a friendship between Xenophon and Cyrus. They only ever briefly exchanged words.[183] From Xenophon, we learn that Cyrus was raised together with his brother and other boys in the court of the Great King. This would be their binding example. They learned there to obey justice and ability above all, and to command.[184] 'What Xenophon touted here as special merits of the Persian educational using the example of Cyrus' childhood presupposes, of course, a form of government other than a democratic model, namely, the (ideal!) monarchy represented by a small aristocratic elite in the leading positions – and it may come as no surprise that Xenophon himself personally sympathised much more with this form of government than with democracy.'[185]

Xenophon particularly emphasises[186] that the young Cyrus was trustworthy and upheld all contracts and agreements. One could basically be assured that he would never cheat or deceive anyone. He also ensured through dissuasive penalties that people could move around unmolested by criminal elements in his satrapy. He created loyal subjects by generously rewarding actions that were in his interest, and considered it fair that people were rewarded for good performance.

Xenophon explicitly stresses (*Anabasis* 1.9.20–28) that Cyrus placed great worth on genuine and long-standing friendship. This had a materialistic-utilitarian basis. It was based on mutual benefit and not on emotional ties. Cyrus always had a strong desire to do good for his friends and to honour them in public.

The Mercenaries

As early as the seventh century, the Egyptian Pharaoh Psammetichus I recruited Greek mercenaries, who later settled in Egypt – in Memphis and Naucratis – after their service was finished. During the Peloponnesian war, there were a large number of mercenaries employed by Greek cities and reinforcing their troops. The Persian satraps fought their battles against each other with the aid of Greek mercenaries. The Persians are even said to have later used these combat experts against Alexander the Great. The mercenaries for Cyrus' campaign were no exception.[187]

'We've seen how Brasidas first recruited, in addition to Spartan perioeci, Greek mercenaries for his march on Chalcidice and Thrace. Athens did the same when they were at war in the northern border areas. In many cases, the mercenaries were recruited from the area of the fighting itself. Unlike the hoplite farmers, the mercenaries were able to fight on rough terrain, camp in remote areas in winter months, and were more knowledgeable of the prevailing conditions than the hoplite citizens. Only by using mercenaries were the commanders able to undertake expansive land-based campaigns where a militia army would be doomed to failure because of its close connections to the polis of the homeland.'[188] The most famous example of this new kind of warfare was Cyrus' army of 10,000 Greek mercenaries, who, after the death of their leader, were led by Xenophon from the Euphrates to the Black Sea, and from there back to Greece where they could be recruited for new mercenary services.

The War Diary

As I stood before him, Cyrus simply said: 'The Pisidians are wild, unruly mountain people who are constantly making trouble for the Great King.' Clearly, he wanted to erase any note of doubt as to the alleged punitive nature of the expedition. 'You understand that I am currently very busy.'

He turned to leave, when Proxenus asked: 'Cyrus, my prince, may Xenophon accompany me? I could use his help.' Cyrus considered for a moment. 'Very well. If you watch out for him, then he may come. I have no special job for him for the moment, though.' He paused, then added: 'That is to say, we will take him along as a scribe to make a written record of our operations. His records will help me to submit an appropriate report to the Great King.'

Happy, Proxenus replied: 'I will take care of it, Cyrus.' Before I had a chance to thank the prince, he had left the room. I was surprised how quickly everything had happened. The honour of helping Cyrus as a scribe would help me to pursue my search for Thucydides greatly. How gladly I would have told this to Philesia!

Proxenus could see my joyful reaction to this important order on my face. 'When this expedition is over, you will be free to stay or return home.'[189]

I thanked my friend. I was glad to come along to Pisidia, even though I did not expect to find Thucydides among the Pisidian bandits. But you never know!

The Departure

The distance between Sardis and Sagalassos in Pisidia was no further than the distance between Ephesus and Sardis. It was a difficult journey by land, but you could access the country by sea if you really wanted to. For a force of more than a thousand men, however, complex and conspicuous preparation was required. These were my thoughts as we left Cyrus' palace.

Proxenus had set up a simple bivouac in his spacious tent for me; it would only be for a night. Xanthus had rolled his mat out next to the tent.

It was already dark when we lay down to sleep. We had eaten and drunk beforehand. Bread and cheese had been served to us by unseen hands on a folding table. The night was quiet.

At dawn, the tents were dismantled and packed into trailers along with our small items of luggage. Then everything started moving very quickly. I now had the opportunity to count the men. There were well over a thousand armed men, and just as many horses. In addition, there were around 200 servants and assistants who had loaded the tents onto the trailers. The harnessing of the stubborn mules was not quite as simple, but they managed it. The convoy was ready to march.

The riders, under the command of Proxenus, waited impatiently. My friend had obviously woken long before I had. When he saw me, he reminded me to always stay near to him when we were on the road.

'We will ride out in front. More people will join us once we leave the city, and will line up behind us. We're ready to go,' he called to me.

I had bought my horse in Sardis a day earlier. After we had arrived, Xanthus took me to a horse dealer he knew well. There were eight horses in the stable. He urged me to hurry, so I had no time examine the animals carefully and had to rely on my first impression. The dealer seemed trustworthy. He also didn't want to lose favour with Cyrus' stable master, with whom he regularly did good business. We quickly came to an agreement.

Then the great door of the palace opened. Cyrus emerged and mounted his steed, which was being held in place by two men. He called out: 'Are you ready?' With one voice, his riders called back: 'We are ready!'

Immediately, we set off, pairs of riders side by side, to navigate the narrow streets of the city. On the vast plains outside the city gate, there were hundreds more riders and thousands of heavily armed men on foot. Every last one of them belonged to Cyrus' army. Most of them had been recruited from Greek cities for a good price. They had survived the Peloponnesian war and were glad to serve the Persian prince. Old enmities and rivalries were forgotten. All of them were hoping for a rich reward after the successful completion of the punitive expedition against the Pisidians.

For a brief moment, I asked myself again whether it was appropriate to bring such a large force down on the Pisidians. Furthermore, it seemed pretty risky to operate with such a large number of men when the terrain was still deep in spring snow. I kept my concerns to myself, though, not even discussing them with Proxenus. Only once did I get carried away with the comment: 'Hopefully there won't be too much snow up there!' My words fell on deaf ears, and I consoled myself with the thought that it grew warmer every day.

My satisfaction that Cyrus had inspired former wartime opponents to take part in a joint task eventually won out. Athenians and Spartans, Boeotians and Thessalians no longer stood against each other. They had a shared objective. In my official war diary, I would later be able to list many more Greek tribes, regions and cities that served in Cyrus' army.

The Ascent

In the first weeks, Cyrus moved south-east with his soldiers in the direction of Pisidia. They crossed the Meander with a bridge of boats. They stayed in Colossae for a week, where they were joined by the Thessalian Menon. He commanded 1,000 hoplites and 500 peltasts armed – as was customary – with only a small shield, a sword, and several spears. Cyrus' army then proceeded to Celaenae. In this large and prosperous Phrygian city, they stayed for a month.

Xenophon had time here to continue work on his diary, which he had given the name *Anabasis*: 'In Celaenae, Cyrus had a fortified palace and a large park full of wild animals, which he used to hunt on horseback whenever he wished to give himself and his horses exercise. Through the middle of this park flows the Maeander river; its sources are beneath the palace, and it also flows through the city of Celaenae. There is additionally a palace of the Great King in Celaenae, heavily fortified and situated at the foot of the Acropolis over the sources of the Marsyas river. The Marsyas also flows through the city, and empties into the Maeander.'[190]

Thus reads Xenophon's entry in the diary. During the army's stay in Celaenae, Xenophon asked the inhabitants many things, including the origin of the name 'Marsyas'. They told him that, according to legend, the source of the river lay at the point where Marsyas challenged Apollo to a competition, and where the victorious god had skinned the satyr Marsyas and hung his hide in a grotto.[191]

The legend they told Xenophon dealt with the invention of the flute by the goddess Athena, who discarded the musical instrument in spite of its beautiful sound, believing it disfigured her face when she blew into it. Marsyas found the flute and coaxed pleasing tones from it. He showed off his art in front of the nymphs, before finally challenging even the god Apollo to a musical competition. The god was victorious, and punished the loser cruelly. This is portrayed in the Roman poet Ovid's *Book of Days* (6.692–

710). In *Metamorphoses* (6.382–400), Ovid also explains the origin of the River Marsyas' name.

In Celaenae, the exiled Spartan mercenary leader Clearchus[192] also added 1,000 hoplites, 800 Thracian peltasts and 200 Cretan archers to the mercenary army. Cyrus then conducted the first comprehensive survey and census of his army. There were now 11,000 hoplites and around 2,000 peltasts under his command.[193]

Then, to everyone's surprise, they continued further north, and a few days later, south-east. Pisidia was obviously no longer the target of the expedition. What was Cyrus planning? That Cyrus was seeking a confrontation with his brother, the Great King, was known – it later turned out – only by the mercenary leader Clearchus. Everyone else, justifiably, felt deceived, but they did not leave Cyrus' army. No one wanted to be seen as a coward. It was not until much later that the mercenaries learned that the Persian satrap Tissaphernes, who had been a massive supporter of the Spartans during the Peloponnesian war, had been following Cyrus' forces, and had grown suspicious. From the outset, he had viewed the preparations for the expedition against Pisidia as far too costly. He had, therefore, taken 500 riders to the court of the Great King to tell him what he had witnessed, and to warn him. Artaxerxes began to prepare appropriate countermeasures.

By now, around three months had passed since the troops had set off from Sardis. The Greek mercenaries sent multiple delegations to Cyrus to demand their agreed payment. He stalled with excuses, and was ostensibly apologetic that he was unable to fulfil the soldiers' legitimate desires. If he had had the necessary funds, he would not have behaved as he did.[194] He was at least able to provide his soldiers with enough food, for as long as the army was still within his satrapy, it was simply requisitioned and the soldiers did not have to buy it with their own money.

Epyaxa

One day, while the troops were stopped in Caystrupedion, a woman came to meet Cyrus. She was Epyaxa, the wife of the Cilician prince Syennesis. She was attended by her bodyguard.[195] After a brief introduction, she explained that her husband had sent her to ask Cyrus not to invade Cilicia. To ensure this, he was prepared to offer a large sum of money. This meant he was finally able to pay his army for the four months he owed them.[196] Morale among the men was greatly improved.

Epyaxa was extremely beautiful. She wore wide silk trousers under a kind of shirt that reached from her chin to her knees and was closed with a delicate ribbon at the neck. Her tiny hat seemed to dance on her blue-black curls like a cork floating on the waves at sea. Her well-formed face was not covered with a veil but she wore – as was the custom in Cilicia – heavy make-up. It made her face appear far brighter than it really was. She was a petite but powerful figure, and resembled the young women in Sparta who did not seek to conceal their beauty because they kept themselves healthy like the Greek athletes through regular exercise and effort, through running, riding and swimming, and were not afraid to expose their skin to the sun.

The Cilician queen stayed with Cyrus for two weeks. There were inevitably rumours about a very close relationship between Cyrus and Epyaxa. She was his mistress for a very long time, and was also able during this time to procure the money for his soldiers.

One day, in Thyriaion, Epyaxa expressed her desire to see the mercenary army.[197] Cyrus ordered the leaders of the individual contingents to arrange the soldiers in battle formation. He visited the native troops first, and then the Greeks as he rode past the rows of soldiers in his chariot. Epyaxa accompanied him in a light carriage. Cyrus then sent Pigres, an interpreter, to the Greek mercenary leaders and gave the order for the entire army to advance. On a trumpet signal, the soldiers began a mock attack. The men charged in the direction of the tents and stalls. The merchants and convoy servants, unaware of the true intent of the manoeuvre, fell into a panic and fled from their wagons and stands. Even the Cilician queen was taken to safety in her carriage. The Greeks, however, returned to their tents laughing.

The woman marvelled at the magnificent display and the discipline of the army, and Cyrus was proud of his mercenaries who had shown their strength and skill so impressively. As a reward, he paid the men extra. For the Greek mercenary leaders and the Persian nobles from the immediate surroundings, he had a feast prepared. It was to take place according to 'Etruscan custom'. Cyrus wanted this feast to pay homage to Epyaxa, as she was a Lydian princess and it was said that the Etruscans had emigrated from Lydia to Hesperia several hundred years ago to found a new, powerful state.

Epyaxa was originally to be married to Cyrus. His father, Darius, who had reigned over the Persian empire for over two decades,[198] had, however, given into the solicitations of the Cilician prince Syennesis and ordered Epyaxa's father to marry her off to Syennesis, despite being fully aware of the deep affection his younger son had for the Lydian princess. Darius, however, wanted to foster close ties with Syennesis and thereby force Cilicia into his sphere of influence. That Cyrus never forgave his father for this decision is understandable. Syennesis gave his young wife – he was almost four decades older than Epyaxa – complete freedom, and accepted that she met with Cyrus whenever possible. It is said that Cyrus had an inconspicuous house on the island of Cyprus where the couple spent many happy days.

Epyaxa's grandmother was, incidentally, Artemisia – the daughter of Lygdamis of Halicarnassus. This remarkable woman participated in Xerxes' campaign against Greece and even fought at Salamis in command of a small fleet, although she tried to get Xerxes to avoid the disastrous battle.[199] Had the Great King listened to Artemisia, he probably would have been victorious over Greece.

So Cyrus insisted on hosting the 'Etruscan feast' for Artemisia's great-granddaughter. The Etruscans – it is said – lived extremely indulgent and immoral lives.[200] They forced their female slaves to serve the men at the feast completely naked. Even the flautists performed naked – except for a bow in their hair. The women who attended the feast were also usually naked alongside the men, and were extremely heavy drinkers. They would order their slaves not only to endlessly refill their wine glasses, but also to pour wine over their naked bodies to cool themselves.

The 'Etruscan feast' that Cyrus and Epyaxa celebrated was, however, as harmless as the Etruscans themselves. With the exception of the female musicians, no one was naked. While much alcohol was consumed, uninhibited lovemaking during the binge was avoided. The Etruscan feast therefore differed very little from a Greek symposium, though there was no witty conversation.

Research for the Diary

The often week-long breaks in marching gave me plenty of time to record what I saw or what others told me in my diary. Even then in Sardis, I bought 'pergament' from a trader from Pergamus, which was very pleasant to write on. I could stow this material in my luggage far better than the fragile rolls of papyrus. This was why the Ionian Greeks in particular – including Herodotus – used these durable goat skins from Pergamus, which were so suitable to write on, for their records.

I took every opportunity to talk with the soldiers and record their observations and experiences. I wanted to learn why, among other things, they were participating in this campaign. Most soldiers – I noted – had joined Cyrus because they were fascinated by his personality.[201] Some had even brought friends and relatives. Some had run away from parents, or left their wives and children behind. They all had one wish: to return rich and healthy, and not stay in Persia forever. Of course I wanted the same thing. I, however, had given myself a particularly difficult task: I was still looking for traces of Thucydides so as not to disappoint Philesia any more than I already had.

But the further we advanced into Persia,[202] the less likely it was I would learn anything about Thucydides. If the Greeks didn't know anything, why should the Persians? Proxenus was probably the only person in Cyrus' army who had even heard of the Greek historian. It was that very reason, however, that compelled me to continue my research. If I returned home empty-handed, I would at least be able to publish and distribute the parts of Thucydides' work which I had previously brought to safety. Additionally, I also intended to use his previous records to complete his work in his style.

Three days later, we arrived in Iconium, the last city in the Phrygian area. We rested there for three days before continuing to Lycaonia and Cappadocia. Even before we left for Tyana, Cyrus bid farewell to Epyaxa and sent her back to Cilicia the quickest way possible.[203]

Menon

The Thessalian Menon and his men were to accompany Epyaxa. He had a total of 1,000 hoplites and 500 peltasts who had joined us in Colossae. Why exactly were they given this task? Was Cyrus particularly trustful of Menon? It was, after all, Epyaxa, and Menon was by no means a model soldier.[204] On the contrary – he was an unscrupulous criminal who would do anything to increase his power and wealth. He was frequently seen with Socrates in Athens and would boast about his 'talent for deceit' and his skill for 'lying for his own benefit' at every opportunity.

He once wanted to borrow money from me. At the time, I was unaware of his perfidy. He said to me: 'I will give you a Thessalian brood mare as collateral. She's worth far more than the amount I'm asking for.'

I asked my father for advice. 'Bring the horse to me and I'll give you the money your friend needs. But only for a short while!'

I handed the money over to Menon. He promised to return the amount in two months with interest.

Two weeks later, however, an old man appeared with his two sons at my father's farm. 'I'm looking for my horse. The mare was stolen in the night from the pasture by Menon and Tharypas, his catamites. There were witnesses. He doesn't even deny the theft. He sent us to you, Gryllus. He claims you bought the horse from him even though you knew it was stolen.'

Gryllus was speechless, but he returned the animal without hesitation to her rightful owner.

The next day, I called Menon out. He said 'Do you see how I fooled you? It was so easy to cheat you and your father! I just want to point that out.' With a sardonic grin, he added: 'Oh, your gold is all gone. You don't have any witnesses to the fact that you ever gave it to me anyway. Aren't you impressed by what a clever rogue I am?'

I despised Menon utterly. I asked myself what Socrates saw in him – among other things, a year before his campaign, he had a talk with him because he had passed himself off as an expert in the matters of virtue, boasting that he had repeatedly held public lectures on virtue and earned a lot of money because of them.[205]

'His false friendships served only to grant him safe access to his so-called friends' assets. Just by looking at the mocking expression on his face, you could tell he considered those who told the truth to be fools. He guarded against people like himself as though he were guarding against heavily armed enemies, but he considered honest and decent men to be weaklings for him to exploit. He would boast outright in public about his ability to cheat and invent lies and laugh about his friends – he went so far as to call decent men 'uneducated'. With powerful men, he did everything he could to play the role of the close friend, unscrupulously elbowing his way into a position of power by slandering his friends. […] He (Xenophon) blamed Menon's corrupt character not only on his disposition, but also on his education; he is portrayed as the model image of a young man reduced by a sophistic education to a contentious cynic who despised from the very depths of his soul the ancient values (which Xenophon held in such high esteem) of piety, sincerity and modesty, and who would often loudly proclaim this fact publicly; he regarded them as pure stupidity and naïveté and whosoever defended them deserved nothing more than to be ripped off. […] Menon embodies the type of sophist student that was probably not rare at the time, whose interest was limited to the radical elements of the teachings, and who failed to genuinely engage with them. It was easy for such 'half-educated' young men to become revolutionaries and uncompromising despisers of traditionalist society, for whose value system they had nothing but scorn and ridicule. Thanks to their intelligence and dialectical education, they were able to achieve their personal goals using methods others would regard as fraud and slander, but they

themselves saw as the legitimate use of their intellectual superiority over the naïve "uneducated". In this sense, Xenophon obviously wants to expose Menon in contrast to Proxenus who – although he had also succumbed uncritically to the promises of the teaching – had survived the old system of values.[206]

Every attentive reader of my diary will have noticed that my portrait of the Thessalian Menon is influenced by Thucydides' analysis of man.[207] In Menon, I found all the negative qualities Thucydides ascribed to people in general. He was living proof of the accuracy of Thucydides' image of man.[208] Many events on our march through Persia also confirmed the historian's observations. In this way, you might say I encountered Thucydides again and again during our procession before and after Cunaxa.

Epyaxa arrived in Tarsus five days before Cyrus. Menon had lost a hundred hoplites while crossing the mountains. It was reported that they had been cut down by marauding Cilicians. Others claimed that the men had become lost in the mountains and died there. When their comrades heard this, they pillaged the city and the castle. Syennesis, the prince, had fled into the mountains. He was, however, willing to meet with Cyrus if he guaranteed him his safety. Epyaxa arranged this.[209] Cyrus once again received money for his campaign.

I could not let go of the question as to exactly why Menon had been allowed to accompany the woman to Cilicia. I appealed to Proxenus. My friend responded without thinking twice: 'He volunteered. Clearchus and the others weren't interested in the task. Cyrus was actually quite happy when Menon volunteered. He knew that Menon couldn't stand women and that he needn't worry about him harassing Epyaxa.'

'I don't understand.'

'There's another reason. Have you ever met anyone as greedy as Menon?'

'No, Proxenus.'

'He hoped to receive a huge reward for bringing Epyaxa safely back to Tarsus.'

'It didn't work out that way though,' I said, gleefully. 'He even lost a hundred hoplites in the mountains!'

'That's right, but aren't we all here to earn money?' asked Proxenus.

'Not I, you know that,' I responded

'I don't believe Cyrus will be ungenerous if you use your daily records to praise him as a great general. He will reward you royally.'

'There's a long way to go until then.'

A Pointless Search?

'How goes your search for Thucydides?'

'If I had any news, you would know about it.'

'Have you spoken with the Thracian traders who joined our convoy yesterday yet?'

'Yes, Proxenus.'

'And?'

'They boast that they know many prominent Greeks. In Abdera, they supposedly even met the philosopher Democritus, and they once apparently ran into Protagoras on the road. They hadn't heard from Thucydides in a long time, though. It seemed pointless to question the Thracian traders any further. The Abderites at least assured me that they would notify me immediately if they heard anything new. I promised them a good reward if they did. They'll find something. I should be happy. And I was happy – who else travels the world like Abderite traders?'

There was nothing else I could say to Proxenus. He seemed to have expected this.

The entourage certainly attracted as many civilians as soldiers. At least it seemed that way to me. I couldn't count them. Each time we passed through a village, some would leave, and yet others would join up with our convoy. People were constantly coming and going. It actually made for very favourable conditions for the flow of news and information. You could find out everything that was happening in the inhabited world if you so wanted, yet nobody had heard anything about an Athenian historian. It was as though he had simply disappeared from the Earth or been swallowed by the ocean. As the days went by, the search began to seem hopeless – I was about ready to give up and say goodbye to Cyrus and Proxenus at the first opportunity I got. From Tarsus – we stayed in the city for twenty days – I would be easily able to find a ship back to Piraeus. Cyrus would certainly be able to find another diarist.

Mutiny

The mercenaries didn't seem to want to move on. There were rumours that Cyrus intended to lead them against the Persian Great King. They hadn't signed up for such a risky venture.[210] Clearchus' soldiers were openly resistant. Clearchus himself was almost stoned to death, but he was able to calm them at the last minute and persuade them to hold a peaceful assembly.[211] Clearchus gave a speech to his soldiers. Xenophon recorded the speech verbatim in his war diary, which he later published under the pseudonym 'Themistogenes'.[212]

The general stood before his men for a long while in silence, shedding bitter tears.[213] They were so surprised and impressed by this not one of them dared say a word. He wept like a defendant in court, where tears were a proven means to appease a judge.

'Men, soldiers: do not wonder that I am distressed at the present situation. Cyrus became my friend. He honoured me when I was exiled from my fatherland and granted me 10,000 darics. I did not use this money for my own purposes, but instead spent it on you. First I led you on the punitive expedition against the Thracians for Greece, driving them out of the Chersonese when they wanted to deprive the Greek settlers of their land.

Then when Cyrus' summons came, I brought you to him, in order that, if he so desired, I might support him. I did this out of gratitude for how he had treated me with respect. Now you do not wish to continue the march with me, and now I have a dilemma: I must either desert you and continue to enjoy Cyrus' friendship, or I must break my word to him and remain with you. Whether I shall be doing what is right, I know not, but at any rate I shall choose you and with you shall suffer whatever I must. No man will be able to say that I, after leading Greeks into the land of the barbarians, betrayed the Greeks and chose the friendship of the barbarians. Since you do not care to obey me, I shall follow with you and suffer whatever I must. I am convinced that you are everything to me: fatherland, friends, comrades; only with you shall I be honoured wherever I may be and without you I would be unable either to aid a friend or to ward off a foe. Be sure, therefore, that wherever you go, I shall go also.'[214] There was no doubt that Clearchus was serious and no longer wanted to follow Cyrus. In secret, however, he remained in touch with Cyrus and told him that he had no cause for concern: everything would soon be rectified.

The soldiers soon realised that they would put themselves in a very difficult position if they refused Cyrus' command. Since they didn't yet know what Cyrus was planning – perhaps the rumours he was marching against the Persian Great King weren't true – they decided to negotiate with him.[215] The prince explained to the soldiers that he intended to take action against the Phoenician satrap Abrocomas, with whom he had a dispute. The Phoenician, who was allegedly just twelve days' march away from Tarsus on the Euphrates, was a loyal follower of the Great King.

Cyrus was only able to sway the mercenaries by promising them a pay increase of one-and-a-half times: 'In Tarsus and later in Thapsacus, the approval of the mercenaries to continue the march against the Great King was basically only gained through financial promises. In fact, the mercenaries only enlisted in the mercenary army in order to make money, and would have done so for any man without any inner commitment to the cause. In this case, they essentially demanded 'danger pay' due to the extreme danger and difficulty of the task ahead of them (cf. 1.3.19).'[216]

Later, it was revealed that Cyrus had also officially requested Sparta's support for his campaign without revealing his true intentions. He claimed at the time that he required Spartan aid to deal with the rebel province of Cilicia.

Then, in Issus, the last city on Cilician ground, thirty-five ships arrived from Peloponnese under the command of a certain Pythagoras. The Egyptian Tamos had accompanied them from Ephesus with twenty-five additional ships. In this way, 700 hoplites were transported to Tarsus under the command of the Lacedaemonian Cheirisophus. He also joined up with 400 soldiers who had left the service of the satrap Abrocomas.

With the arrival of Cheirisophus, whom Cyrus had 'invited', as it were, along with his impressive forces, it was gradually becoming impossible to overlook the possibility that Sparta was increasingly interested in supporting Cyrus by any means possible against the Great King. Obviously, Spartans made up the majority of the Greek mercenaries who could be cheaply bought after the war and now even the Spartan fleet was involved in the adventure. Although most of the mercenaries still believed the undertaking would be a geographically limited campaign, Cyrus had long since agreed with the Spartan leaders the means by which the Spartan side could bring about the violent change of power of Persia.

No Turning Back

The Cilician city of Issus was one – although not my last – chance to return to Greece by means of a merchant ship. I had three days to think about it.[217] I was under no obligation to Cyrus. Abandoning Proxenus, however, I could not justify. Cyrus had, however, made a special point of putting me in charge of the war diary. But had he given me this task because there was nothing else for me? Nothing exciting had happened so far which warranted being recorded for posterity (unless you counted the heavy losses Menon's soldiers had suffered in the Cilician mountains due to his thoughtless actions). How would I explain abandoning the search for Philesia's father, though? I had justified my participation in this adventurous campaign with my hope of finding news about Thucydides.

We crossed the border into Syria without meeting any resistance. There were numerous merchant ships in the Phoenician port town of Myriandrus. We stayed there for seven days, plenty of time to find a ship home, but I immediately banished the thought from my head once I witnessed Xenias the Arcadian and Pasion the Megarian embarking on a ship back to their homelands.[218] *Cyrus felt betrayed by these men. He had trusted them for a long time and given them many important tasks. Because of their past achievements, he refrained from following them and bringing them to justice in spite of his disappointment. I even believed he accepted the two Greeks' flight, since it gave him the opportunity to demonstrate his generosity. In a speech to the mercenary leaders, he explained that while it would not have been difficult for him to follow the men, he would not do so, for no one should be able to claim that he exploited people if they stayed with him and punished them when they wished to leave. Instead, they should be allowed to leave, but with the knowledge that their actions were worse than his.*

These words had their desired effect. Anyone who had previously doubted whether or not they should continue now no longer had any concerns.[219] *This was also true for me. I would never have forgiven myself if I had simply fled like Xenias and Pasion. In my diary, I explained the change of mood towards Cyrus' imposing superiority, which he had in actions and behaviour demonstrated for all to see.*

The True Goal of the Expedition

When the mercenaries had reached the Euphrates in Syrian Thapsacus, Cyrus called his Greek generals together – Xenophon was permitted to accompany his friend Proxenus in his capacity as war diarist – and bluntly informed them about the 'journey' to Babylon. What had been long suspected or even known was finally official.

For posterity, Xenophon wrote: 'Cyrus summoned the generals of the Greeks and told them that the march was to be to Babylon, against the Great King; he directed them, accordingly, to explain this to the soldiers and try to persuade them – yes, that was the word Cyrus used – to follow. Immediately, the generals called an assembly and informed the soldiers.'[220]

Once again, they felt betrayed by their leaders and protested loudly. Some even threw stones. Gradually, however, the commotion died down. The men stood together in small groups, wondering what to do now. Finally, they asked their captains to communicate the conditions under which they were prepared to move to the commanders. The captains decided to send the eldest among them to speak with Clearchus: Lycarius of Sparta, a prudent and level-headed man. He set out with three other captains. Without hesitation, they informed Clearchus of their soldiers' decision 'We are prepared to march on if our payment is increased – as when we marched with Cyrus to his father without having to fight.'[221]

Clearchus and the other generals relayed their soldiers' demands to Cyrus. In addition to their rightful pay, he promised each individual a large reward when they reached Babylon. He also wanted to ensure that they returned safely to the Ionian coast after successful completion of the campaign. The soldiers – with few exceptions – gave up their resistance.[222]

Information Gathering

Since I had been put in charge of the war diary, I had tried to keep in touch with the simple soldiers. In numerous interviews, I tried to understand the mood of the army and get to know the difficulties, wishes and expectations of the men. They were normally very happy to talk with me. It meant a change to their otherwise uneventful and monotonous days. I regretted it all the more that I hadn't found any who hadn't wanted to follow the majority of the mercenaries on the banks of the Euphrates. I also never figured out the reason behind it. There were, of course, the sick among them who simply couldn't, and others – as I suspected – who simply wanted to stay in Thapsacus for whatever reason. Still others wanted to return to the sea to hire a merchant ship, because they had been promised riches there.

Sometimes, I was able to bring the interpreter Pigres along to hear what moved the Persian soldiers. I, incidentally, also intended to return someday without the interpreter and try to learn the Aramaic language, as it was the common language in the Persian world. With an understanding of Aramaic, I would be able to read the inscriptions the satraps made to announce the commands of the Great King.

Of course, I learned a lot about Cyrus and the individual commanders through my interviews with the soldiers. I was, after all, trying to capture character profiles which were as vivid as possible in my diary.

Increasingly, Cyrus himself seemed to be gaining a reputation as an exemplary military leader. He possessed all the virtues that distinguished a leading figure. Everyone with whom I spoke agreed that he had a particular ability to find the right balance in all situations. He was in that respect like Cyrus the Great, the founder of the Persian Empire. I believe I could even say that there was no man, after the older Cyrus, who was more suitable and more deserving of the throne than our Cyrus.[223]

Of course, I took every opportunity to question the people in the convoy. Communication was not particularly difficult. The tradespeople travelled the world and had a good command of the Greek language.

Cyrus was delighted when Proxenus told him about my detailed research. He also let me know that I could turn to Glus, the son of the Egyptian Tamos, if I ever had specific questions. Glus belonged to his inner circle. He had Cyrus' full confidence, and was extremely well informed of everyone's background. If he wanted to reward or praise someone in particular, he would send Glus, who would express appreciation on behalf of the prince and hand over the appropriate reward. This is what happened when Menon was the first to cross the Euphrates with his soldiers.[224]

Crossing the Euphrates

The Euphrates was vast – you could scarcely see across it – and crossing it was extremely difficult. With the help of a local fisherman, however, a ford was found. The water was low enough at this ford that the water only came up to the soldiers' knees. The horses and chariots crossed without much difficulty. No one – according to the people of Thapsacus – had ever forded the river before. The soldiers had been forced to, because Abrocomas had burned all of the boats on the shore while they marched to the Great King in order to hinder Cyrus' progress.

Then a divine miracle occurred: the river receded before Cyrus as though paying homage to the future king, falling to its knees before him. All those who still doubted Cyrus fell silent.

No one was seriously injured while crossing the Euphrates. There were only a few minor accidents. At one point a heavily loaded wagon became mired in a mud hole. It had come off the track trying to overtake a wagon in front. Stock was lost. We went without salt for a few days. That was all. The crossing of the river did, however, last from dawn until long into the night. The mood was good, though. A huge fire was made from driftwood gathered during the crossing, so we were able to dry our clothes and everything else.

The Convoy

On the banks, flies and mosquitoes swarmed around men and animals alike. A few had mesh nets with which they could protect themselves. Some wrapped themselves in sheets and blankets to ward off the pests. Wood was collected everywhere and many fires burned deep into the night. The fires were the only protection against the intolerable nuisances.

Because I reached the other bank of the river faster than most of the others with the help of my horse, I had chance to look back at the vast procession. The convoy consisted of hundreds of two and four-wheeled carriages pulled through the river by horses, mules and oxen. No one could say how many people marched in the convoy. Their numbers seemed to me to exceed the number of hoplites. It was a mixed bunch. It was as though an entire city had joined our procession. Many men had brought their wives and even their children. Every one of them hoped to find a better life for themselves and their families in Persia.

In Sardis, there had been only a few wagons. They transported supplies, tools and weapons, equipment for backers, saddlers and blacksmiths. These workers were not mercenaries, but were paid as though they were, because keeping them happy and motivated to continue following Cyrus with the promise of substantial rewards was equally as important. In the long run, without their aid, the army of hoplites would not have been able to continue marching.

Traders and prostitutes, artists and entertainers, medics and preachers all joined as if from nowhere. They all hoped to earn huge amounts of money. To maintain order, even judges were appointed to settle the inevitable disputes. There were unwritten laws that mainly served to protect the personal property of the people.

There were no punishments. Whoever had caused any damage simply had to make up for it. Sometimes an offender was chased off with a beating or a stoning like a mangy dog. No one wanted anything to do with a thief or a cheat. If they left anything behind, it was distributed among the convoy. Although there was plenty of evidence of stealing and cheating, there was also evidence of people being helpful. There were doctors who treated the sick without asking for payment, and traders who gave to the needy.

Cyrus and his Greek strategists only intervened in the lives of the people in the convoy when the interests of the soldiers seemed at risk. This could be the case when food intended for the soldiers was dragged from the wagons in the night, or when someone was suspected of being a spy for the Great King. Clearchus had impaled several Syrians on stakes on the banks of the Euphrates whom he had accused of having spied for Tissaphernes. Many were shocked by this cruelty. Only Proxenus, however, dared to confront him: 'Clearchus, are you sure that the men you had killed were really spies? You had them brutally murdered merely because you suspected them on account of accusations made by a few despicable individuals – people who should face justice. You didn't even interrogate them. Why didn't you bring an interpreter?

Clearchus

Clearchus,[225] who had long had a reputation for maintaining the discipline of his soldiers with severe punishments, replied, shrugging: 'Even if they had been innocent, the sight of them will scare anyone else considering betraying us.'

The execution of these alleged spies showed the cruelty of this mercenary leader – on Clearchus' orders, the bodies were to remain on the stakes until they rotted, or fell off themselves, or were eaten by animals. His behaviour also seemed to have something to do with his deep-seated hatred of the lives and activities of the 'blowflies', as he called the members of the convoy. The Syrians had been impaled as representatives of these 'vermin'. From the humourless look on his face, he would just as soon have repeated the whole gruesome action. This could explain his endless hatred of everything that afforded pleasure. He seemed to despise everything that brought joy, with the exception of the bloody frenzy of battle. He couldn't, however, prevent the acrobats, the snake charmers, the storytellers from the orient, the dancers, the musicians and the magicians who tried to break up the monotony of the lives of the soldiers from performing.

Although Clearchus was a good soldier and an excellent commander, he could only ensure the obedience of his men with extreme severity. He acted on the principle that a soldier had to fear his superiors more than his enemies. 'His behaviour seems to me to be the behaviour of a man who loves nothing more than war – he was like a more passionate 'Philopolemus'. Although it was possible for him to enjoy a quiet life, he would rather take risks and expend effort fighting in wars. He could have enjoyed great wealth in safety, but he wasted his money on war like others wasted money on a lover or for cheap pleasure. Such was his love of war. He seemed to be fitted for war in that he was fond of danger, ready by day or night to lead his troops against the enemy, and self-possessed amid terrors, as all who were with him on such occasions agreed. He was regarded as a kind of born leader. […] He knew how to teach the people around him that he was to be obeyed. […] When his soldiers faced the enemy, there were good reasons why they were so efficient. They were confident in the face of the enemy, and their fear of punishment at Clearchus' hands kept them in a fine state of discipline.'[226]

News of Thucydides?

During our five-day stay in Thapsacus on the Euphrates, I continued my investigation into the whereabouts of Thucydides. Alas, I was again unsuccessful. Every chance I had, I asked the newcomers about him. I even searched in the city itself. I found no signs of him.

Then, one day – we were already approaching the abandoned city of Corsote – three men from the convoy came to me. They came from the island of Thasos and claimed to have something for me – but only for appropriate compensation.

I settled on a trade, but how much I paid them would depend on the reliability of their information. The Thasians agreed. They claimed that a man from Abdera had heard from a friend in Amphipolis that Thucydides had been sighted in one of his gold mines a few weeks back. He had been trying to settle a dispute among a group of miners.

'What were they fighting over?' I asked.

'Something about poor working conditions. The workers refused to crawl into a tunnel. Risk of collapse!' answered the Thasian.

'What did he do then?' I asked.

'He ordered the foreman to reinforce the tunnel. He managed to calm the workers down.'

'How do you know it was really Thucydides?'

'People said the owner or the tenant of the mine settled the dispute personally.'

This answer did not convince me. Even if the name 'Thucydides' had been dropped, it by no means meant that this was the man I was searching for. It could be the other Thucydides, son of Melesias and political opponent of the great Pericles,[227] from Thrace, or anyone else by the name Thucydides.

I thanked the Thasians and gave them a small amount of money, even though there was nothing I could do with their information. Even if it really had been Thucydides, it wasn't impossible that this argument between his miners had been settled before he had returned from exile, and not recently.

The Thasians swore blind that the events had taken place just a few weeks earlier. I expressed my doubt that these men could only ever have heard of one man named Thucydides. They explained: 'Thasos isn't far from the mainland. We were looking for good work, and it was recommended that we try the mines on the mainland, since there's always something to be earned there. That's when the conversation turned to the dangers of mining, and so on.'

That didn't sound completely absurd. Under normal circumstances, I would certainly have investigated this clue, but I couldn't imagine that he could have disappeared to Thrace just like that without at least leaving a message. He would surely have had to say something to his daughter Philesia, not to mention Gryllus and myself – and why would he have so casually left his books and papers with us? They were so important to him.

None of it made sense. Something else must have happened.

I was gradually realising that it was utterly impossible to find a trace of the historian from the banks of the Euphrates. Again and again I had asked our carriage driver if he had noticed anything out of the ordinary when Thucydides had told him, outside Critias' home, that he would not have to wait for him, or to come back to pick him up later. At the time, he had only wondered why Thucydides had disappeared so quickly through the doorway, as through dragged through by force by an invisible hand. But why? Had Critias actually been at home? Was it possible someone else had been waiting there for Thucydides?

Question after question without answer. Then there was the fire that had shortly thereafter burned the author's house to the ground.

Years later, I learned that a human body, burned beyond all recognition, had been found in the basement of the burned house. No one ever made a connection between the ghastly discovery and the owner of the house, although this assumption was not entirely unfounded. The banishment prevented me from continuing my search in Athens.[228]

Downriver

There was no respite from the flies and mosquitoes on the banks of the Euphrates. Not even at night. Herodotus reported that the Egyptians took the following measures against mosquitoes[229]: *they climbed towers at night and slept up there. Because the mosquitoes couldn't fly high enough, it was then possible to sleep in peace. But we had no towers on the banks of the river. We didn't even have the nets people used to fish during the day and then put up around their beds at night at our disposal.*

Many men suddenly came down with a fever. Some doctors claimed that the mosquitoes had brought the disease. Others blamed the contaminated waters of the great river. Some even said that the Persian satrap Abrocomas had had the water poisoned during his flight to Babylon. Many claimed to have seen the bodies of animals and humans floating in the water.[230] *They thereafter ordered that any water taken from the river must be boiled before drinking. So no one died of thirst for fear of the water.*

After a few days, just as quickly as it had come, the fever disappeared. Was it perhaps a warning sign from the gods? Many of us brought offerings of thanks to Zeus, Apollo and Asclepius. Small alters were built out of stones and twigs where prayers could be murmured. Cyrus and his Persian compatriots prayed to an invisible god, the creator and ruler of the world, who had been announced to them by a certain Zoroaster. This was the grandson of the last king of the Median Empire Astyages, related through his mother to the reigning king and then, of course, also to Cyrus.

After the prayers, Cyrus had the entire camp 'purified' – the people, the animals, the weapons, the luggage. The magician touched everything with the sacred fire of a white burning torch. They wanted in this way to prevent another flare-up of the fever.

Cyrus also incidentally had an Egyptian doctor amongst his followers, who was convinced that most diseases could be prevented if you paid attention to the cleanliness of the body, and the purity of what you ate. He claimed it was better to eat the pure meat of a freshly slaughtered dog than the leg of a cow that had died from a disease of some sort. To the followers of Zoroaster this was a horrible idea, as for them the dog is a sacred animal.

The Greek doctors did not disagree with the Egyptian, but they also looked down on the practice of interpreting illness as a sign from the gods. The mosquitoes and putrid water were the causes. Nevertheless, they could have nothing against thanking the gods for the resolution of the fever.

I bought some roots from a Syrian doctor who had joined us in Thapsacus that were to be cooked and pressed, resulting in a liquid you could rub into your skin. This substance was effective against the mosquitoes, but it smelled terrible. One would therefore have to decide whether to ward off mosquitoes or men. Even the horses were put off by the smell, and would snort when the disgusting stench invaded their nostrils.

After we passed the Araxes, the Euphrates' tributary, we stayed close to the banks of the great rivers as best we could. We would often have to march through uninhabited land for days. The land was as flat as the ocean. There was only fragrant grass and many shy animals – wild donkeys, ostriches, bustards and gazelles. Sometimes I would go along with the Persian riders to hunt,[231] but we were rarely successful. The animals were simply too fast for us. I was only once able to catch a wild donkey in my net. The ostriches were impossible to catch or kill.

After a few days, on the other side of the Euphrates, we saw the city of Charmides.[232] We wanted to resupply there with the most essential provisions. In order to cross the river, the soldiers who were to buy the provisions sewed waterproof bags from skins and blankets stuffed with hay. On these floating cushions, they would cross the river and pick up the food.

Orontes

Just before the army crossed the border into Babylonia, there was a peculiar incident. There were many Persians in Cyrus' entourage who more-or-less willingly obeyed the Persian prince and would, depending on the situation, do everything to prove their loyalty to Cyrus or the Great King. Cyrus perceived precisely the danger in this.

He once settled a dispute between Clearchus and Menon – after Proxenus had been unsuccessful in his attempts to keep them apart – with the following words: 'Clearchus, and Proxenus, and all you other Greeks who are here, you know not what you are doing. As certainly as you fight with one another, you may be sure that on this very day I shall be instantly cut to pieces and yourselves not long after me! Once we show weakness, all these Persians whom you see before you will become more hostile to us than are those who stand with the Great King.'[233]

Shortly thereafter, the Persian satrap Orontes appeared on the scene.[234] He approached Cyrus' army with 2,000 horsemen, but kept his distance to await further developments. He wanted to leave the question of which side he supported open for as long as possible, unable to judge whether Cyrus or the Great King would emerge victorious. Obviously, he wanted to be on the side of the victor. Accordingly, he offered to support Cyrus, while simultaneously sending a letter to the Great King to assure him of his loyalty. His double-dealing was discovered quickly enough when the messenger handed Cyrus the letter meant for the Great King. Orontes was exposed as a traitor. He was summarily tried and sentenced to death. After he was discharged, however, he disappeared and was never seen again dead or alive. Nobody could say if or how he died. Some suspected something else. A grave was never found.

'Cyrus did not expect genuine solidarity and dedication from his local troops, who had been forcibly called up for an undertaking in which they were not in the least bit interested. […] Orontes' behaviour corresponds with Cyrus' realistic assessment (1.5.16). Probably only a few of the Persian dignitaries who inevitably accompanied Cyrus on his march gave his coup attempt a real chance. Some may have wondered how he would back out at the last moment and give the Great King a sign of his loyalty to avoid further punishment. Orontes' plan, which had apparently developed spontaneously out of the situation, had been cleverly thought out. In particular, it seemed important to keep the actual arrival of Cyrus' army in Babylonia a secret as long as possible in order to be able to exploit the element of surprise.'[235]

Orontes' clear political interests were not his only schemes. His double-dealing was probably due to the fact that he – as Xenophon reported[236] – wanted to destroy Cyrus after earlier having made war with him and then been reconciled. Nevertheless, it was understandable that Cyrus would accept the offer of aid from his old enemy – he wanted to avoid his plans being announced too early in Babylon, and he needed any support he could find for his final battle against the Great King.

Growing Tension

Tension grew. The decisive battle was imminent. Cyrus ordered a final inspection of his army and had the number of his solders estimated. He was convinced that the Great King would attack imminently.[237] He summoned the generals and captains and delivered a powerful speech to strengthen their fighting spirit: 'Men of Greece, I did not bring you here because I did not have enough Persians to fight for me. Rather, I believe that you are braver and stronger than many Persians. This is why I enlisted you. You will now have the chance to show that you are worthy of the freedom you possess, and for which I congratulate you, for you should know that I would chose this freedom over everything else I own.'[238]

Whether or not Cyrus' claim that he would rather be a free Greek than a rich Persian was serious is not the question here. What was impressive was his reference to the freedom the Greeks had once fought for. With this reference, he hoped to make the Greek mercenaries think of their heroic ancestors who had successfully repelled the tremendously superior Persian forces almost a hundred years ago in several major battles. The Battle of Marathon (490 BC), in which the Greeks defeated the Persian invaders, obliged the descendant of the victorious warriors to do the same. It was also to be expected that the Persians saw this similarly, and were afraid of the Greeks' courage and willingness to fight.

Cunaxa and the Consequences

Cunaxa was 500 stadia[239] north-east of Babylon. Xenophon avoided mentioning the name of the place in his diary. He wanted to forget it. For Xenophon, this was a place of failure and painful memories. Cyrus fell in the battle. His dead body was mutilated, his head mounted on a spike.

Xenophon describes as much of the battle as he saw: 'The Greek mercenaries remained undefeated and ready to fight.[240] They were unable, however, to stop the Persian soldiers from conquering Cyrus' camp. In the general chaos, even the prince's harem fell into the hands of the marauding hordes.[241] The women – among them Greek women – were captured and taken to Babylon. Only one of them escaped and sought protection in the successfully defended camp of the Greek mercenaries.'

It wasn't long before a delegation from the Great King and the satrap Tissaphernes appeared at the gates to accept the mercenaries' surrender. A single Greek was among them: Phalinus of Zakynthos, an advisor to Tissaphernes.[242] When the negotiators were within earshot, they demanded the commanders come to them and accept the orders of the Great King. He was the victor, because he had killed Cyrus. The Greeks should surrender their weapons immediately to avoid a worse fate. Clearchus firmly rejected this. It was not for the victor to surrender his weapons. Proxenus, sarcastically, asked whether the Great King would consider the weapons as the spoils of victory or a gift between friends.

Phalinus replied on behalf of Artaxerxes[243]: 'The Great King is without a doubt the victor because he has slain Cyrus. Who else would challenge his reign? You also now belong to him – he has you in his country, enclosed by two impassable rivers.[244] He can bring against you a multitude of men so great that you could not slay them even if he were to give you the opportunity.'

To everyone's surprise, Xenophon suddenly rose to speak – in his diary, he gave himself the pseudonym 'Theopompus of Athens',[245] which can be approximately translated as 'the messenger of god'. 'Phalinus, at this moment, as you see for yourself, we have nothing other than our weapons and our valour. If we keep our weapons, we imagine that we will be able to demonstrate our valour, but if we give them up, that we must expect to also give up our lives. Do not suppose, therefore, that we shall give up our only possessions without a fight. We would much rather fight you for them.'[246]

These confident words fit very well with the active initiative Xenophon demonstrated some time later when he dragged the soldiers out of their despair and despondency after the loss of their leader and spurred them to action.[247]

Phalinus, however, responded with sarcastic laughter: 'Why, you talk like a philosopher, young man, and what you say is quite pretty; be sure, however, that you are a fool if you imagine that your valour could prove superior to the King's might.'[248]

Phalinus once again demanded that the Greek mercenaries give up their weapons, but the Great King actually seemed to want to relent. He seemed ready to call a ceasefire. After some time, another Persian delegation arrived to begin negotiations.[249] Tissaphernes even claimed he was prepared to offer the Greeks safe passage to the coast of Asia Minor.[250] However, the Great King first wanted a convincing reason why they had ever taken up arms against him in the first place.[251]

They discussed the matter carefully, and eventually had Clearchus the Persian give the following report:

'We did not come together to make war on the Great King. Cyrus, however, found many pretexts, as you also are well aware, to bring us here and take you by surprise. Then, however, we saw that he was in serious danger. We did not want to shame ourselves before the gods and men by betraying him, since in the past we were all eager to receive his good grace and the benefits that came with that. However, Cyrus now lies dead, and we neither challenge the Great King for his throne, nor is there any reason why we want to harm his territory. We want to return to our homes, if no one should molest us. If anyone seeks to injure us, we shall try with the help of the gods to retaliate. If, however, anyone is kind enough to do us a service, we shall not, so far as we have the power, be outdone in doing a service to him.'[252]

Tissaphernes' Betrayal

The Great King then allowed the Greeks to retreat unmolested. Tissaphernes was allowed to accompany the men to the coast of Asia Minor. The Greeks were, however, despite this agreement, very mistrustful of the Persians and their entourage.

One day – they had reached the River Zapata – Clearchus asked the satrap to talk. He agreed, and tried make it clear that he was no threat to the Greeks.[253] Even Clearchus let himself believe that Tissaphernes had no evil intentions for the Greeks. He even hinted that he was secretly pursuing the same objectives as Cyrus.

Nevertheless, Clearchus wanted to make certain and find out if there was perhaps a traitor who shared the Persians' cause among the Greeks. For this reason, he agreed to accept Tissaphernes' invitation to come to his camp with five generals and twenty captains to discuss the matter with the Persians.

Only a few soldiers thought it dangerous when their captains and generals accepted this invitation. Tissaphernes was not to be trusted. These warnings fell on deaf ears.

When the Greek officers finally stood before Tissaphernes' tent, they were called in, whereupon they were immediately disarmed and captured. Clearchus was killed immediately. The rest were brought to Babylon and executed there[254] – save for Menon. He was never heard from again.

A Dangerous Situation

After the loss of our generals and captains, we were practically handed to the enemy defenceless. We found ourselves in the middle of Persia surrounded by enemies. We had to contend constantly with robberies and we had few opportunities to obtain food. We were 10,000 stadia from home[255] and we had no one to show us the way. Huge rivers blocked our way. Most of us were overcome with crippling terror. No one could understand what had happened. Tissaphernes' breach of promise made us realise we could expect nothing but death or slavery from the Persians.

It quickly became obvious to me that the Persians could not be allowed to see our general despondency. We had to continue to present them with the image of a powerful army.

Through my numerous conversations with the soldiers in the previous months, and because of the general acceptance of the importance of my role as the writer of the war diary – Cyrus had pointed out this fact and asked everyone to support my work often enough – I had, over time, earned the respect of the people. My courageous stand against Phalinus had had an effect too. I was respected. This was why I felt obliged to offer the men a few words of encouragement in this present emergency. I had to convince them that we couldn't give up, despite the apparent hopelessness of our cause.

I had learned something very important from my sophist teachers: Words can be used as weapons to achieve an objective. Now the emergency had come. The sophist rhetoric had to prove that it could also save lives by inspiring people to take decisive action. Even against Phalinus, I had succeeded in speaking out against the Persians taking our weapons. I had explained that we could only prove our bravery while still in possession of our weapons.[256] Now it was time to confirm this assertion.

The gods once again came to my aid: they sent me a dream.[257] I was aware that dreams could contain divine signs, so I quickly got to work on the art of interpreting them and distinguishing the meaningful dreams from the meaningless dreams. I have tried to do this time and time again.[258]

I tried again now. My father Gryllus' house was struck by lightning and was bathed in a bright light. At first, I believed this to be the sign of a great fire, and jerked violently awake – but this was not the case.[259] The light had been sent by Zeus. It was a sign of hope. It could, however, also mean something bad: we were completely surrounded by fire and could not escape. The Great King had prevented out escape.

What a dream actually wants to say, however, arises from thoughts one has immediately after waking from that dream. I asked myself:

'Why do I lie here? The night is wearing on, and at daybreak it is likely that the enemy will be upon us. If we fall into the Great King's hands, what is there to prevent our living to behold all the most grievous sights and to experience all the most dreadful sufferings, and then being put to death with insult? Why should I continue waiting? I must do something!'[260]

I no longer felt that I was here because I had been cheated. I didn't even blame Proxenus. He had been betrayed himself.[261]

I called the captains of my dead friends together, because I knew them best, and shared with them the thoughts that had been aroused by these god-sent dreams. Without them, I probably never would have had the impetus to call on the Greek mercenaries not to give up and to fight for their survival. But it was not me that saved them in the end, as it was later said, but Zeus, who sent me the dream.

Xenophon's Determination

The 'living evidence of the logical train of thoughts which triggered Xenophon's dream while he still lay in bed was, for him, proof of the powerful meaning of the god-sent dreams, but for today's reader it is also an understandable representation of an "awakening experience" that has moved a man from lethargic resignation to his fate, to sudden, energetic action. The first reasoning led logically to the notion that the Greeks, who had previously been so driven by their salvation, must now organise their defence against the Persians' expected attack before dawn if they did not want to – though sheer idleness – invite a dishonourable death. Then – understandable given the general lack of a clear plan – he considered his own person. In fact, only three original generals remained in the army.'[262]

However, these three generals were as disturbed as the rank and file soldiers. Even the experienced Spartan general Cheirisophus had nothing to say in this situation, marked as it was by paralysing horror. Hence Xenophon felt called to action by his dream. 'Here, he gives us a better insight into his thinking. Even where he did not record in his diary the reasoning put forward in the form as we read them, they still represent a plausible reconstruction of his assessment at the time. Presumably he magnified his own role; it must however be noted that he was the one who first moved Proxenus' lochages to energetic action, and later inspired other officers to the same with their help, thereby creating the conditions for an orderly retreat. That this required numerous speeches, debates and votes is a reflection of reality, but also of the fact that Xenophon had mastered the art of speech like no other in this army, and that he owed his by now recognizable influence on events in no small part to this art.'[263]

The Election of the General

I said nothing to the men that they didn't already know themselves. 'The Persians are superior to us in every way[264] and their sole aim is to destroy us. But the gods are on our side. The Persians broke the oaths they swore to them, and we are far superior to them when it comes to enduring cold, heat, exertion and deprivation. The most important thing, however, is that the strength of the gods gives us better fighting spirit. Let us now ask others to resist. If you want, then I shall follow you, but if you want me to lead you, then I will not plead youth as an excuse.'[265] My speech had a profound effect. The soldiers regained their courage. They remembered their abilities. They realised how important it was to want to survive. It was no longer a question of showing bravery to some paymaster. It was a matter of endurance.

Then everything moved very quickly. 'Xenophon should lead us!' called one of Proxenus' men. 'Xenophon was friend to our dead commanders. He should take their place. That is the duty of a friend!'

I did not argue, but I had called for the men to oppose fate, and promised them that we would overcome all difficulties. Now I had to put my words into action.

This proposal should be voted on as in the Athenian assembly, the Ecclesia. I wanted to be elected correctly, and I was elected.

Today I realise that I could have scared the veteran lochages away with the declaration that I was ready to lead them, but the actual outcome was completely different: The battle-hardened men were ready to recognize the writer of their war diary, who had held no other rank in the army, as their superior. At the time, I thought to myself that the officers were especially impressed by my energy and that they were happy to be rid of the annoying problem of having to designate a commander from within their own ranks.

Immediately, the men gathered for a general assembly. I was asked once again to make a speech. Above all, I appealed to the imperative duty of the officers to lead the soldiers by good example. I also demanded that the lost leaders be replaced with new elections to restore order and discipline. As I had before the lochages, I invoked our moral superiority, which made us invulnerable, before the soldiers.

After my speech, the Spartan Cheirisophus took the floor and thanked me. He made sure that my suggestions were put into action without further discussion. My public recognition by the Spartans meant I was accepted into the circle of commanders. I had become Proxenus' legitimate successor.[266]

Now we had to act as quickly as possible. The objective was clear. We didn't just want to survive, but to return home. The direct route to Sardis and Ephesus was blocked to us. It would have been child's play for the Persians to prevent us from taking this path. My plan was to take the path north, along the banks of the Tigris, to the Pontos Euxeinos – the 'Hospitable Sea'. This would also be dangerous, but we had no other option.

My tactical objective was to avoid surprise attacks, or at least successfully defend against them. Furthermore, I also had to find a food supply for several thousand soldiers. There were two options in this respect: either we could buy supplies at any given market place, or we could simply commandeer them as we passed through villages. We had to expect resistance. Conflict also threatened the water sources. In arid areas like this, water was not easy to come by. The remaining convoy had to be protected from attacks. We couldn't afford to lose tents, food for the horses and valuable materials. However, procuring food in the villages for some kind of compensation was not out of the question: I thought on the art of our doctors and the expertise of our craftsmen. We could pay for the necessary food with their services.

The New Role

After his election as Proxenus' successor, Xenophon once again convened an assembly of the army in order to inform them of how they were to proceed. Outfitted in his new Athenian armour, he once again expressed his certainty that the Greek mercenaries could survive anything with the help of the gods if they now proved their determination and vigour.

At these words, a man sneezed, and all who heard it thanked the gods for this positive sign.[267] In his diary, Xenophon wrote:

'I was lucky that at the moment I invoked the aid of the gods, one of the men sneezed loudly, sending the troops into a religious frenzy.' Because sneezing was considered a good omen by which a god announced his aid, Xenophon asked the soldiers to immediately make offerings of thanks. Thus, he gained the support of the entire army. He could not have wished for a better start to his new role.[268]

Xenophon repeatedly pointed out that he always allowed the men to vote – as in the Athenian public assembly – and repeatedly bolstered the courage of the Greeks by reminding them of the tremendous achievements of their ancestors.[269]

Extraordinary Leadership Skills

The fact that Xenophon referred to successful Persian wars of the past is remarkable for several reasons. His listeners were mercenary leaders and mercenaries who did not join Cyrus for patriotic reasons or to fight for their fatherland. Mercenaries were and are not patriots. One must therefore ask whether the memory of the victories against the Persians had any real emotional value. Xenophon at least wanted to remind the mercenaries that a numerically inferior army had defeated a powerful opponent.

After the loss of their leaders, the mercenaries weren't only afraid of being exterminated or enslaved – they could also no longer expect to be paid. Moreover, Xenophon's performance is all the more impressive if we consider that mercenaries tend to become unruly or terminate their services if their expectations are not met. He had not only particular organisational skills and natural leadership, but also strong self-confidence and outstanding rhetorical talent, which gave him remarkable authority.

Even while Cyrus was still alive 'discipline very quickly became a problem, which one can follow through various stages: Not only did the mercenaries behave inappropriately as they passed through cities and other properties, but they also complained about Cyrus and his strategists, their behaviour bordering on mutiny on several occasions. These elements – which had largely been filtered out of the polis' world – could hardly integrate into a new community or society, and did not want to put aside their own desire for wealth and a comfortable life (which often carried with it the expectation of having a family or slaves), in favour of deliberate discipline. The leaders found it difficult to reason with them, particularly since punishments for criminal behaviour could only be applied in a limited fashion. Rather, they preferred to work […] by means of persuasion, and particularly by making many promises. […] Loyalty to 'comrades' was in short supply – in crucial moments of crisis, everyone was looking out for themselves. If Thucydides demonstrated that with the outcome of the Syracusan expedition, or with specific events of the Decelean war, then Xenophon, with the arrival of the Ten Thousand in Trebizond, demonstrates it even more clearly; it is especially surprising, since the main dangers had been overcome, but it is well established in the character of the mercenary that even then they were still thinking about personal gain (even if it meant piracy), returning home, or entering into new, more favourable mercenary jobs. Basically, the extensive human failure of the mercenaries was not only due to the situation of the war, the instability of the way of life, or generally bad relations with their employers. Rather, most of these soldiers were driven to it by their background and character – they were without exception downgraded elements: adventurers, exiles, criminals, or people who had found no livelihood in their homelands. People who had been torn from the normal fabric of society.'[270]

Given this background, it is understandable that Xenophon emphasizes his reasons for participating in the march of the Ten Thousand.[271] He was no mercenary and originally had no military function. He was simply a man who had accepted a friend's invitation for a trip to Persia. It was very important to him to stress that he was not a socially uprooted adventurer like the ordinary mercenaries. He emphasized the importance of his role in his diary, choosing his words with great care.

Tactical Changes

The esteemed Spartan general Cheirisophus now asked the soldiers to accept Xenophon's suggestions. They complied. Without complaint, they destroyed everything they didn't need. Only then could maximum marching speed be achieved. This made sense to everyone.

Xenophon had the marching formation of the army changed. The Ten Thousand would no longer march in a long and therefore easy-to-attack column, but in a compact square. The remaining convoy stayed in the middle. The hoplites formed a border to the square to the extent the terrain allowed. To be able to fend off attacks better, Xenophon created a more nimble unit. He was able to put together a contingent of around 200 hurlers and a small cavalry of at least fifty men.

While the Ten Thousand made good progress at first over the relatively friendly terrain, only occasionally being attacked by Persians and suffering hardly any losses, the situation changed radically once they entered the land of the Carduchoi.[272] Xenophon records in his journal that the mercenaries were fighting almost constantly while they travelled through the mountains. They had to endure worse than the battle against the Great King and Tissaphernes.[273]

Lied to and Cheated again

Before we reached a point where we could see the sea,[274] we had to endure yet more difficulties with the inhabitants of the region. The Scythians, for example, gave us a guide to lead us through their territory unmolested, but then demanded we plunder and burn villages on the way. The Scythian ruler had obviously not sent us this man out of kindness: we were to subjugate or even exterminate his disobedient subjects. We had let ourselves be misused for a bloody punitive campaign.

Even though we had become used to committing violence to survive and repel attacks in recent months, many of us found it unbearable to be lied to and cheated once again. It is obviously the nature of man to exercise power by lying and cheating. Later, when I read Thucydides' history book, it became clear to me that our actions not only in the Scythian lands, but also before and after Cunaxa, confirmed the message of his work. We experienced numerous examples of wickedness and inhumanity, and we even committed some ourselves. We were both victim and perpetrator. What, according to Thucydides, happened in the murderous war between Athenians and Spartans we once again brought to pass – on a smaller scale – in the months before and after Cunaxa.

Thucydides was right. As long as man exists, there will be monsters.[275] The difference between the great Peloponnesian war and the march of the Ten Thousand lies only in the number of people involved and who experienced war as 'a violent teacher'.[276] This was an easy game, because one only needed to release the natural disposition of man. In a time of peace, these evil attributes could not emerge and exert their power.

The march of the Ten Thousand therefore did not afford me the opportunity to search for Thucydides, but by the end, I found I had begun to understand his thoughts. It was not until I finished my war diary in Skillus,[277] however, that I understood them fully.

Although we failed at Cunaxa without being beaten, the constant fear of the Persians remained our driving force for the months thereafter. Thucydides was right here, too. 'After the Persian war – according to the Athenians – we saw ourselves forced to expand our dominion to its current size chiefly out of fear, next for honour, and finally for our own benefit.'[278]

These were also the driving forces for us followers of Cyrus.

A First Look at the Sea[279]

Then something remarkable happened. The leading edge of our troops had reached the mountain Theches.[280] When they first reached its peak and saw the sea, they broke out into shouting and cheering. We in the rear guard, hearing this, feared a surprise attack. A group of possible attackers had pursued us for some time now. They wanted to take revenge on us for setting their villages on fire and killing or capturing some of them after we had lured them into an ambush. We had seized around twenty shields made from the densely furred skins of freshly slaughtered cattle.

As the shouting quietened and the advancing soldiers tried to run to those shouting as quickly as possible, I leapt on to my horse and galloped past the others with Lyrcius and the other riders to render assistance. Moments later, we understood what the soldiers were still shouting with all their might: 'Thalatta! Thalatta![281] *The sea! The sea!'*

Finally at their Destination

The circle closed itself. The followers of Cyrus had finally reached the end point of their expedition. Their 'odyssey' was – at least for the time being – over. Home was in sight. It didn't matter if it was the Black Sea or the Mediterranean. The main thing was that it was a sea, because 'She is our great sweet mother'.[282]

'With the Black Sea, on whose shores are located many Greek colonial cities, the Hellenic homeland greeted from over the mountains that homesick, almost-lost crowd. Because they had suffered from homesickness since the death of Cyrus and the murder of the strategist, at the mercy of the foreign land "unable to sleep for grief and longing for their native states and parents, their wives and children, whom they thought they should never see again." (3.1.3). [...] They trust the sea as familiar and more so because it meant a return home, safety, an end to all their troubles. When the Greeks held a general assembly of the soldiers near the sea near Trebizond, Leon of Thurii captured the general sentiment when he said: "I am tired by this time of packing up and walking and running and carrying my arms and being in line and standing guard and fighting. What I long for now is to be rid of these toils, since we have the sea, and to sail the rest of the way, and so reach Greece stretched out on my back, like Odysseus." (5.1.2) What he probably alludes to here is the last phase of the wanderings of Odysseus, wherein Odysseus is brought home on the Phaeacian ship and arrives in Ithaca, the sight of which he had long dreamt of, in his sleep. However, the awareness of having survived an 'odyssey' gave hope not only of a favourable outcome to the adventure, but also of fame that 'reaches unto heaven'. (*Od.* 9.20). That these literary reminiscences got their message across effectively is shown in Xenophon's exhortation to the mercenary leaders before the beginning of the return march, where he mentions the first adventure of Odysseus with the lotus eaters, when the fellowship forgot their way home through sheer enjoyment (3.2.25).'[283]

In the *Odyssey*, Homer describes the departure of the Phaeacians mentioned by Leon of Thurii as follows[284]: 'But when they had come down to the ship and to the sea, straight away the lordly youths that were his escort took these things, and stowed them in the hollow ship, even all the food and drink. Then for Odysseus they spread a rug and a linen sheet on the deck of the hollow ship at the stern, that he might sleep soundly. Then he too went aboard, and laid down in silence. Then they sat down on the benches, each in order, and loosed the hawser from the pierced stone. As soon as they leaned back, and tossed the brine with their oarblades, sweet sleep fell upon their eyelids, sleep which could not be broken. [...] Thus she sped on swiftly and clove the waves of the sea, bearing a man the peer of the gods in counsel, one who in time past had suffered many griefs at heart in passing through wars of men and the grievous waves; but now he slept in peace, forgetful of all that he had suffered.'

Xenophon deliberately sought to tie his *Anabasis* to Homer's *Odyssey*. Before the Phaeacians, he even mentioned the lotus-eaters. Just by mentioning Odysseus' adventures, he calls attention to the 'oriental fairytale world' of the Persian empire, which even the followers of Cyrus seemed to have in their minds at times. There are other connections to be drawn between the wanderings of Odysseus and the return march from Cunaxa to the Black Sea.[285] The fact that Xenophon – like James Joyce after him – used Homer's *Odyssey* as a mythical foil for his description of events after Cunaxa is obvious.

Cairns of Gratitude

The shout of joy 'Thalatta! Thalatta!' caused a powerful movement. Everyone rushed forward, driving the pack animals and horses to speed. When they reached the lookout, they hugged each other and shed streams of tears – even the generals and the captains. They then gathered stones and piled them up into a huge cairn. Then they lay the hides of freshly slaughtered cattle upon it, their walking sticks and their captured shields, and the guide himself, who had shown them the way, cut these shields to pieces and called the others to help him.[286]

One could only speculate at the time why the soldiers built such cairns. They wanted to build a monument to their deeds and their suffering that would stand for all time.[287] These stones, however, also represented the weight that was lifted from their shoulders when they looked back over everything they had achieved.

What Happened Afterwards

By March 401 BC, the expedition in Sardis had begun. The period between the actual *Anabasis* and the Battle of Cunaxa in September was seven months. Then Xenophon's odyssey began. They reached the Greek colony of Trebizond after eight months – fifteen months' travel in total – in May of the year 400 BC.

The majority of the soldiers arrived in Byzantium in October 400 BC. They were not admitted into the city, and Xenophon could not prevent them from simply forcing their way in and plundering.[288] The army showed its first signs of breaking down. Many set off alone to return home.[289]

Fortunately, the Thracian Seuthes made an appearance.[290] He offered the destitute followers of Cyrus food and pay, if they agreed to support him in his own military conflicts. As usual, the soldiers discussed this among themselves. A vote was called and everyone agreed to follow Seuthes.

Although the followers of Cyrus were able to complete the operations in Thrace successfully, they were initially denied their promised reward. The soldiers got their money only after tough negotiations.

Xenophon led the now greatly reduced troop back to Asia Minor. In Pergamus, the home town of Gongylus, the followers of Cyrus decided to make a raid against the Persian Asidates. The option, to plunder and extort ransom money, was suggested to Xenophon by Hellas, the mother of the reigning prince Gongylus.[291] He described this last campaign in detail before the handover of the troops to the Spartan commander Thibron. The attack, which was undertaken with approximately 1,000 men but was otherwise completely pointless from a military point of view, was apparently intended to offer the followers of Cyrus an opportunity not to return home empty-handed.

The surprise attack on the secure estate of the wealthy Asidates was initially unsuccessful.[292] The followers of Cyrus were able to retreat only with great difficulty and after suffering heavy losses. Only two days later did the unsuccessful raid turn into a successful one. Xenophon ordered the entire army to march in the night in order to feign the Greeks' withdrawal. Asidates attempted to flee to safety with his family, but was captured by Xenophon and his men, whereupon he was forced to give up all his belongings.[293]

In March 399 BC, Xenophon put the 5,000 men of the combined troops under the command of the Spartan Thibron in Pergamus,[294] who immediately engaged them against the Persian governors Tissaphernes and Pharnabazus. Xenophon apparently remained the commander of the followers of Cyrus. This is supported by a note in his account of Thibron and Dercylidas' military operations in Asia Minor.[295]

Xenophon was probably replaced by the Lacedaemonian Herippidas in 395 BC,[296] in order that he could take on a new role serving Agesilaus. In *Anabasis*, he writes only that he left Asia Minor with the Spartans to march to Boeotia.[297] The successful battles against the Boeotians, Athenians, Argives and Corinthians on the planes of Coronea followed.[298] Xenophon proudly mentions the outstanding bravery of 'his mercenaries' under the leadership of Herippidas.[299]

He had no idea at the time, but this adventure in Coronea would prevent him from returning to his homeland for decades.

Notes

Abbreviations: An. = Anabasis; D. L. = Diogenes Laërtius; Hell. = Hellenica; Her. = Herodotus; Cyr. = Cyropaedia; Mem. = Memorabilia; Oec. = Oeconomicus; Th. = Thucydides; Xen. = Xenophon

1. cf. Christian Meier: *Athen. Ein Neubeginn der Weltgeschichte*, Munich 2004.
2. cf. Gregor Weber in: Kai Brodersen (ed.): *Virtuelle Antike. Wendepunkte der Alten Geschichte* [Virtual Antiquity. Turning point of Ancient History], Darmstadt 2000, 11–23.
3. 'On the Thirty' Karl-Wilhelm Welwei: *Das klassische Athen. Demokratie und Machtpolitik im 5. und 4. Jahrhundert* [Classical Athens. Democracy and the Politics of Power in the Fifth and Fourth Centuries], Darmstadt 1999, 247–257.
4. Weber 2000, 20.
5. On the 'pathology' of human behaviour and attitude in extreme situations: Th. 3.82 f.
6. 'they began tearing the walls down to the music of flutes' (Hell. 2.2.23).
7. Hell. 2.2.24.
8. Hell. 2.2.20.
9. Hell. 2.2.1 ff.
10. D. Lotze: *Lysander und der Peloponnesische Krieg* [Lysander and the Peloponnesian War], Berlin 1964. cf. Plutarch's biography of Lysander.
11. Hell. 2.2.20.
12. Initially involved the second walls, the construction of which began in 459 BC. They linked Athens with Piraeus (approx 7 km), the others ran from Athens to Phalerum (approx 6 km). A third wall was later built parallel to the wall between Athens and Piraeus. Together with the wall around Athens and Piraeus, 26 km were defended. See also Meier 2004, 367 ff.
13. Hell. 2.3.1 ff.
14. Th. 8.68.4.
15. Harmosts were the military commanders employed to assert their interests in conquered cities.
16. Thrasybulus was a decorated Athenian commander and democratic statesman. His services in the liberation of Athens from the domination of the Thirty is described in 2.4.10–22.
17. Hermann Bengtson: *Griechische Geschichte von den Anfängen bis in die römische Kaiserzeit* [Greek History from its Origins to the Roman Empire], Munich 1965, 231

18. Hell. 2.3.11.
19. Hell. 2.3.50–56.
20. Hell. 2.4.
21. Critias even had Socrates forbidden from speaking with or asking questions to people under the age of thirty. In Mem. 1, 2, 29–38 Xen. attempts to illustrate that the relationship between Socrates and the Thirty was extremely tense.
22. The fragments of his work can be found in the collection of pre-Socratics of Diels/Kranz (No. 88).
23. Th. 8.92.
24. Hell. 2.3.48.
25. Hell. 2.3.48.
26. Hell. 2.3.49.
27. Hell. 2.3.31.
28. as did Aristophanes, Frösche 534 ff.
29. Constitution of the Athenians 28.5.
30. Hell. 2.3.
31. Th. 8.68. cf. Cicero, *De oratore* 2.22 and *Brutus* 7.
32. Hell. 2.3.21.
33. Hell. 2.3.21.
34. Xenophon also identifies himself in An. 2.4.19 as a 'young man' who remained sensible in critical situations.
35. Xen.'s reproduction of Critias' and Theramenes' speeches (Hell. 2.3.24–49) makes it very likely that he heard both himself.
36. Hell. 2.3.25.
37. Otto Lendle: *Kommentar zu Xenophons Anabasis (Bücher 1–7)* [Commentary on Xenophon's Anabasis (Books 1–7)], Darmstadt 1995, 148
38. An. 3.1.47
39. An. 5.3.6. Hell. 4.3.15–21. Xen. Agesilaus 18.
40. cf. Lendle 1995, 315 f. On Xen.'s exile: Hans Rudolf Breitenbach: *Xenophon von Athen* [Xenohpon of Athens], Stuttgart 1966 (= RE IX A 2), 1575 There is no doubt in Breitenbach's eyes that Xen.'s participation in the Battle of Coronea in the year 394 BC fighting for the Spartans was the reason for his exile and not his participation in Cyrus' expedition. Also, from An. 5.3.7 it is clear that the exile was only imposed when Xen. returned from Asia with Agesilaus (396). cf. Lendle 1995, 315.
41. It is entirely possible that Xen. based the depiction of women in his work on his own wife's traits: So, for example, the mention of the Armenian prince Tigranes' wife could contain echoes of Xen.'s wife Philesia (Cyr. 3.1.36: 41. 43. cf. Eduard Schwartz: *Fünf Vorträge über den griechischen Roman* [Five Lectures on the Greek Novel], Berlin 1943, 70).
42. Pausanias 5.6.5.
43. D. L. 2.53.
44. D. L. 2.59.

45. Breitenbach 1966, 1573.

46. Luciano Canfora: *Die verlorene Geschichte des Thukydides* [The Lost History of Thucydides], Berlin 1990, 93 Canfora draws on Marcellinus' 'Life of Thucydides' (17 and 31–34) from the fifth/sixth century BC

47. Holger Sonnabend: *Thukydides* [Thucydides], Hildesheim 2004, 15 f.

48. cf. Th. 4.108.

49. Th. 3.36; 4.21.

50. Th. 6.55.1.

51. cf. Th. 1.22.

52. Th. had indeed not finished his historical work, but was still working on it after the end of the Peloponnesian war. This applies e.g. for Pericles' speech (2.60–64). According to Th., the defeat could be attributed to, among other things, the fact that the Athenians did not take Pericles' advice into consideration (65).

53. cf. Manfred Fuhrmann: 'Ein Mordfall? Luciano Canfora über Thukydides' [A Case of Murder? Luciano Canfora on Thucydides], in: *M. F.: Europas fremd gewordene Fundamente. Aktuelles zu Themen aus der Antike* [Europe's Alienated Foundations, Current Issues from Antiquity], Zürich 1995, 32–35. Canfora appears to think Xen. is Th's murderer.

54. Hell. 2.3.

55. It is entirely possible that Xen. was born in 424 BC.

56. Lenaia was celebrated over several days in honour of the god Dionysus. A parade and performance of comedies in a dramatic competition were essential parts of the festival. (Aristotle, Constitution of the Athenians 57.1)

57. Lysander, born ca. 455 BC, was instrumental to the Spartan victory in the Peloponnesian War. He was responsible for the Thirty seizing power in Athens.

58. Hell. 2.1.27 f. Diodorus, *Universal History* 13.106.

59. These characterisations of the two politicians can be found in Mem. 1.2.12.

60. Apart from Th. (books 5–8 of his work) and Xen. in Hell. (esp. book 1), Plutarch's *Biography* from the first century BC is an important source of information on Alcibiades.

61. Helmut Berve: *Die Tyrannis bei den Griechen* [The Tyranny in Greece], Munich 1967, 208 f.

62. Alcibiades is characterised in detail by Ferdinand Broemser: 'Größe und Niedergang im Geschichtswerk des Thukydides' [Size and Decline in the Historical Work of Thucydides], in: *Der altsprachliche Unterricht* [The Classical Language Lesson] 9, 3, 1966, 30–71.

63. This is in sharp contrast to Pericles statement in the funeral oration (2.37.1).

64. Broemser 1966, 54.

65. Plato, *Apology* 24b and Xen. Mem. 1.1.1; also D. L. 2.40. Robin Lane Fox: *Die klassische Welt. Eine Weltgeschichte von Homer bis Hadrian* [The Classical World. A History of the World from Homer to Hadrian], Stuttgart ³2010, 193: Socrates did not 'ruin' the young people, he 'was guilty only in that he had not taught them better'.

66. Mem. 1.2.
67. Apology 32b.
68. Hell. 1.6.27 ff. and 1.7.
69. Apology 32c–d.
70. On the reasons for the democratic Socratic process: Jürgen Malitz: 'Sokrates im Athen der Nachkriegszeit (404–399 v. Chr.)' [Socrates in Post-War Athens (404–399 BC)], in: H. Kessler (ed.): *Socrates. Geschichte, Legende, Spiegelungen. Sokrates-Studien II* [Socrates. History. Legend. Reflections. Studying Socrates II], Kusterdingen 1995, 11–38. Frédéric Pagès: *Frühstück bei Sokrates. Philosophie als Lebenskunst* [Breakfast with Socrates. Philosophy as Hedonism], Darmstadt, undated, 31 ff., talks of 'Socrates, the collaborator'. Under the regime of the Thirty, one (not Socrates) showed 'true citizenship' by going into exile.
71. Malitz 1995 points out this possibility.
72. On the regime of the Thirty, which was initially generally welcomed and which then degenerated into a reign of terror: Aristotle, *Constitution of the Athenians*, 35–40.
73. Aristophanes' *The Clouds* premièred in Athens in 423 BC.
74. E. Schmalzriedt in: *Kindlers neues Literatur- Lexikon* [Kindler's New Literature Lexicon], München 1988, Vol. 1, 679.
75. Fragments of the pre-Socratics 80 B 1.
76. Dieter Lau: *Der Mensch als Mittelpunkt der Welt. Zu den geistesgeschichtlichen Grundlagen des anthropozentrischen Denkens* [Man as the Centre of the World. On the Intellectual-Historical Basis of Anthropocentric Thought], Essen 2000, 34 f. cf. Rainer Nickel: *Besitzen und Gebrauchen. Spielarten einer Gedankenfigur vor und bei Aristoteles* [Ownership and Use. Varieties of a Figure of Thought Before and By Aristotle], Marburg 2012.
77. The fictitious date would then be 415 BC at the end of the inter-war period 421–415 BC.
78. Th. 2.35–46.
79. Th. 2.39. On the Epitaphios: Broemser 1966, 30–71.
80. cf. Lendle 1977, 20.
81. Briefly but vividly described by Albin Lesky: *Geschichte der griechischen Literatur* [History of Greek Literature], Bern 1971, 513
82. The war is named after the Spartan King Archidamus, who held supreme command at its beginning.
83. 1.76.2; 4.61.5; 5.105.2.
84. cf. Bruno Bleckmann: *Der peloponnesische Krieg* [The Peloponnesian War], Munich 2007. Herwig Görgemanns: 'Macht und Moral. Thukydides und die Psychologie der Macht' [Power and Morality. Thucydides and the Psychology of Power], in: *Humanistische Bildung* [Humanist Education] 1, 1977, 64–93. cf. Werner Jaeger: *Paideia 1*, 496–513, esp. 500 ff.: Th. gave a blatant display of pure power reason with the Melian dialogue.

85. Skapte Hyle was a city in eastern Macedonia (Thessaly) in the Pangaion hills. There were gold mines in close vicinity to Skapte Hyle (Her. 6.46), which later fell into Athenian possession. Th. supposedly owned a gold mine, wrote his historical work and was also murdered here (according to Plutarch, *Cimon* 4).
86. Plato, *Phaedrus* 230d.
87. Jaeger, *Paideia* 3.247.
88. Aristophanes, *Peace* 571–579.
89. On the Olympic victory Alcibiades fought for and won in 416 BC. Th. 6.16.2.
90. According to Th. 2.22, Pericles avoided open confrontation with the Peloponnesians in the early stages of the war even though they, for example, occupied and devastated the area of the Acharnians in northern Attica, only two hours from Athens. Pericles secured the city and allowed only individual actions against the enemy.
91. 403 BC
92. Xen. lived in Skillus from approximately 388 BC.
93. Breitenbach 1966, 1679, also establishes that Xen. lived through the events as an eyewitness.
94. In winter 404/403 BC
95. The Odeon was a covered concert house, much smaller than a usual theatre.
96. Xen. mentions this episode in Hell. 2.4.26.
97. Xen. Hell. 2.4.19.
98. Since 423 BC
99. Th. 2.47–54.
100. 424/423 BC
101. Th. 4.102–108.
102. Th. 4.106, 3 ff.
103. Homer, Od. 1.32 ff.
104. cf. e.g. Hell. 6.4.3.
105. An example: Hell. 7.5.12 f.
106. 422 BC
107. Th. 5.3 ff.
108. 421/-413 BC
109. 424 BC
110. 432 BC
111. 416 BC Th. 5.84–116.
112. Th. 5.90. possibly wrote this sentence after the actual defeat in the year 404 BC. However, the categorical imperative is suspended during war.
113. Th. 5.16.
114. Th. 5.18 f.
115. Breitenbach 1966, 1670.
116. cf. Hell. 5.4.1.
117. cf. 7.2.1.
118. On Hell.: Breitenbach 1966, 1569–1928.

119. Th. 3.36.6.
120. Cleon is the 'most violent citizen' of the city, the war on the other hand is merely a 'violent teacher' (3, 82, 2).
121. The Knights was performed in 424 BC and won first prize.
122. Paphlagonia lay on the southern coast of the Black Sea. Its inhabitants were considered primitive and uncultured. There were many Greek colonies on the coast, such as Sinope, the home of Diogenes the Cynic.
123. Th. 5.16.1.
124. Th. 3.42–48.
125. Th. 3.50.
126. Meier 2004, 562 f. cf. Alfred Heubeck: 'Gedanken zu Thukydides' [Thoughts on Thucydides], in: Friedrich Hörmann (ed.): *Die alten Sprachen im Gymnasium* [Ancient Languages at Grammar School], Munich 1957, 115–129.
127. Th. 3.41–48.
128. They led the so-called 'Melian dialogue'. Th. 5.85–113.
129. Heubeck 1957, 126.
130. Th. 5.89.
131. Th. 3.42.1.
132. Th. 3.44.
133. Th. 3.44.4.
134. Th. 3.46.4.
135. Th. 5.111.4.
136. Th. 1.76.3 f.
137. Heubeck 1957, 127.
138. Th. 3.46.4.
139. Heubeck 1957, 129.
140. Th 4.81 highlights the Lacedaemonian Brasidas' just and modest appearance and his noble bearing in the war.
141. cf. Cyr 1.2.7.
142. Th. 1.22.4.
143. 410 BC
144. 404 BC
145. An. 7.8.2.
146. The monthly wage of a Greek hoplite in Cyrus' mercenary army was one daric (named after the Great King Darius I).
147. An. 7.8.6.
148. The Munychia was the citadel which served as protection for the harbour.
149. Bengtson 1965, 231 f. The most important source of information for these events is Hell. 2.4.10–22.
150. Hell. 2.4.20 ff.
151. Hell. 2.4.2. – In the Roman author Cornelius Nepos' (ca. 100–25 BC) 'Life of Thrasybulus' (1.2 and 2.4), the reader should draw a direct connection from the Tyranny of the Thirty in Athens to the balance of power in Rome at the time the

biography was being written (35–32 BC). Thrasybulus – according to Nepos 2.4 – did not find the popularity he expected in his preparations for his coup, as even at that time, men spoke of freedom with more bravery than they fought for it (8.2.4). It is reasonable to assume that Nepos was criticising even Cicero's largely passive behaviour in the face of the threat to the old republic or Caesar's senatorial aristocracy. In a letter, Cicero himself recalls Thrasybulus and characterises his actions as 'perhaps better' than his own adaptation to the political situation. At the beginning of his biography of Thrasybulus (1.2), Nepos determined that many had wanted to free their homeland from just one tyrant, but that few had been able to. Thrasybulus, however, was able to free his country from under the yoke of The Thirty. For Nepos, he was not only a role model for patriotism (8.1.1), but also for intelligence and bravery, for he gave the order not to hurt the fleeing supporters of the Thirty, because he believed it just and proper that his fellow citizens be spared. Thrasybulus' behaviour after the civil war was also noteworthy: at the height of his power, after the peace treaty was agreed, he passed a law preventing anyone from being punished or prosecuted for their past actions. The Athenians called this law the 'amnesty law'. If Nepos praises Thrasybulus here for actually applying the amnesty law, then it must be assumed that he also wanted to suggest this behaviour to the victor in the Roman civil war. Maybe Thrasybulus' biography should have been a 'mirror of princes' for Octavian. In his speech 'Pro Marcello', Cicero had already praised Caesar's clemency and flexibility in reinforcing his policy of reconciliation. Cicero possibly anticipated Caesar's murder a year and a half later – on 15 March, 44 BC. Therefore, only Octavian received the opportunity to provide the extensive construction and renewal that Cicero expected from Caesar. In this respect, the importance of the Pro Marcello speech extends far beyond its original purpose and may also have encouraged Nepos in his attempt to contribute to the renewal of political morality.

152. Hell. 2.4.10–22.
153. Hell. 2.4.30–39.
154. Hell. 2.4.19.
155. The Delphic oracle was also mentioned in Homer's *Odyssey* (8.79)
156. Cyr. 8.2.10 ff.
157. This is how Xen. describes the activities of an efficient lady of the house in his *Oeconomicus*.
158. Oec. 7.32 ff.
159. An. 1.1.11; 2.6.16.
160. D. L. 2.55.
161. An. 3.1.4.
162. On Proxenus: An. 2.6.15–20.
163. cf. Raimund Schulz: *Athen und Sparta* [Athens and Sparta]. Darmstadt 2005, 125 ff. Cyrus became involved towards the end of the Peloponnesian War. Th. 2.39. Hell. 1.5.1–10. Cyrus' contribution was significant to the Athenians' defeat.
164. Her. 5.54 indicates that the road from Ephesus to Sardis is 540 stadia long, or approximately 100 km.

165. Sycophants were professional purveyors of slander. They primarily caused trouble in the fourth century BC earning a lot of money. They were used for false testimonies and espionage.
166. Xen. tells the Hercules myth in Mem. 2.21–34.
167. An. 3.1.7.
168. cf Breitenbach 1966, 1774.
169. The Thirty were ousted in autumn 403 BC; Cyrus' expedition began in May 401 BC. Xen.'s journey to Persia began about ten days earlier.
170. This applies for the prehistory of the Peloponnesian War. Th. 1.89–146,
171. He reigned from 465 to 424 BC.
172. Artaxerxes was the older brother of Cyrus. He reigned from 403 to 359 BC.
173. Th. 8.68.2.
174. One of the most prominent Greek physicians in the service of Persia was Ctesias from Cnidus, the personal physician of the Great King Artaxerxes II. He was also the author of a novel-like history of Persia from its beginnings to 398/7 BC. (Persica). He participated in the Battle of Cunaxa under the Great King: An. 1.8.26 f. He also treated one of the Great King's wounds. Her. 3.125 and 129 ff. also mention the successful physician Democedes of Croton who served Darius (reigned 521–486).
175. The short story of the 'Widow of Ephesus' has many variations and was recorded in the Roman author's Satyricon 111 f. It was, however, no doubt a story that had been told for centuries at that point because of her salacious character.
176. An. 6.1.23. cf. 3.1.13 f.
177. Her. 1.86.
178. In An. 1.2.2 Xen. reports that his military action against the Pisidians was merely a distraction from his actual plan – the coup against his brother.
179. An. 3.1.4.
180. Her. 1.136.
181. Ivo Bruns: Das literarische Porträt der Griechen im fünften und vierten Jahrhundert vor Christi Geburt [The Literary Portrait of the Greeks in the Fifth and Fourth Centuries BC] Berlin 1896, 142 ff., correctly points out that Xen. was uncritical in his description of Cyrus. Thus, Xen. sees no problem in Cyrus committing high treason against his brother, the legitimate ruler.
182. An. 3.1.8.
183. An. 1.8.15 ff.
184. In Cyr. 1.2.2–16, Xen. goes into detail on the Persian system of education.
185. Lendle 1995, 78.
186. An. 1.9.7–10.
187. Wilhelm Bernhard Kaiser: 'Zur Anabasislektüre' [Reading Anabasis], in: AU 3, 3, 1957, 37–51, esp. 37–40 on „griechische Landsknechte' ['Greek Mercenaries']. H. W. Parke: Greek Mercenary Soldiers from the Earliest Times to the Battle of Ipsus, Oxford 1973. Also the chapter on the Ten Thousand.
188. Schulz 2005, 143.

189. cf. An. 3.1.13 f.
190. An. 1.2.7 f.
191. The roman poet Ovid tells the Marsyas legend in *Metamorphoses* 6.382–400 and *Fasti* 6.692–710.
192. On Clearchus, who had already made a name for himself as the Tyrant of the Byzantium: Helmut Berve: *Die Tyrannis bei den Griechen*, [The Tyranny in Greece] München 1967, 214 f. Xen. conceals Clearchus' tyranny in his honourable obituary (An. 2.6.1–15). cf. Hubert Trümpner: 'Klearchos, Militarist oder Soldat? Ein Beitrag zur Politischen Gemeinschaftskunde' [Clearchus, Militarist or Soldier? A Contribution to Political Social Studies], in: *AU* 10, 3, 1967, 5–20; Edgar Klauk: 'Die Charakteristiken des Klearchos, Proxenus und Menon in Xenophons Anabasis' [The Characteristics of Clearchus, Proxenus and Menon in Xenophon's Anabasis] (II 6, 1–29), in: *AU* 10, 3, 1967, 21–39.
193. An. 1.2.9.
194. An. 1.2.11.
195. On the travelling activities of high-ranking Persian women cf. the book accompanying the exhibition *Pracht und Prunk der Großkönige – Das persische Weltreich* [Pomp and Circumstance of the Great King – The Persian Empire] in the Historical Museum of the Palatinate in Speyer, Stuttgart 2006, 93 ff. Women had a much stronger public presence than Greek women cf. ibid 89.
196. An. 1.2.12.
197. An. 1.2.14.
198. Darius ruled Persia from 424 to 404 BC.
199. Her. 8.68.
200. Athenaeus 12.517d.
201. cf. An. 6.4.8. Xen. apparently undertook a systematic survey. cf. also Egon Römisch: 'Xenophon' in: *Griechisch in der Schule. Didaktik, Plan und Deutung* [Greek in School. Didactics, Planning and Interpretation], Frankfurt 1972, 65–84, esp. 73 f.
202. The Persians had an extensive road network: Josef Wiesehöfer: *Das antike Persien. From 550 BC to 650 AD.*, Munich/Zürich 1994, 115–119.
203. An. 1.2.20.
204. An. 2.6.21–29. Xen. may have modelled his portrayal of Menon after Th's *Pathology*, in the same way he provides examples of 'pathological' human behaviour in *Anabasis*.
205. cf. Plato, Menon 80b.
206. Lendle 1995, 141 f.
207. Th. 3.82 f.
208. cf. Breitenbach 1966, 1643 f.
209. An. 1.2.26.
210. An. 1.3.1.
211. An. 1.3.29.
212. In Hell. 3.1.2, Xen. points out that he published *Anabasis* under a pseudonym – probably in order to demonstrate as much objectivity in his representation of events as possible. cf. Plutarch, *De gloria Atheniensium* 345 E.

213. cf. Kaiser 1957, esp. 48 f.

214. An. 1.3.3–6.

215. An. 1.3.20.

216. Lendle 1995, 33.

217. An. 1.4.1.

218. An. 1.4.6 ff.

219. An. 1.4.8 f.

220. An. 1.4.11.

221. An. 1.4.12.

222. An. 1.4.12 f.

223. Cyrus' personality is described in detail in An. 1.9.7–31.

224. An. 1.4.13–17.

225. Xen. portrayed Clearchus An. 2.6.6–15.

226. An. 2.6.1–15.

227. More about this other Th. can be found in Plutarch's biography of Pericles, esp. ch. 8.

228. Xen. was probably sentenced to exile as a 'traitor' to his home city in 394 BC because he fought on the Persian side at the Battle of Coronea.

229. Her. 2.95.

230. Strabo 15.3.16 ff. claims that the Persians would usually not urinate into the river, nor would they wash in it or throw anything dead into it.

231. in An. 1.9.6, Xen. mentions that Cyrus was an enthusiastic hunter and that he loved the dangers of hunting wild animals: 'He was once attacked by a bear. He did not tremble, but instead charged the bear. He was torn from his horse and wounded. He still bears the scars – but in the end he killed the bear.' He showed great courage with this act.

232. An. 1.5.10.

233. An. 1.5.16.

234. About Orontes: An. 1.6.1–11.

235. Lendle 1995, 50 f.

236. An. 1.6.1.

237. An. 1.7.1.

238. An. 1.7.3.

239. Cunaxa lay between the Euphrates and the Tigris. The exact location is unknown. It was probably located 90 km (500 stadia) north-east of Babylon. On the Battle of Cunaxa: Otto Lendle: 'Der Bericht Xenophons über die Schlacht von Kunaxa' [Xenophon's Report on the Battle of Cunaxa], in: *Gymnasium* 13, 1966, 429 452. – Plutarch, *Artaxerxes*, chapter 8, mentions the Battle of Cunaxa in 3. 9. 401. He praises Xen's description: An. 1.8.8–29.

240. An. 2.1.4: 'We have defeated the Great King; no one still fights against us.'

241. An. 1.10.2 f.; Lendle 1995, 80.

242. On Phalinus: Lendle 1995, 92 ff.

243. An. 2.1.11.

244. Phalinus refers here to the Euphrates and the Tigris.
245. An. 2.1.12. Only in 3.1.4 does he introduce himself under his real name. Also in Hell. 3.1.2, Xen. uses a pseudonym when referencing his *Anabasis*: Themistogenes.
246. An. 2.1.12.
247. An. 3.1.11–25.
248. An. 2.1.13.
249. An. 2.3.17.
250. An. 2.3.18.
251. An. 2.3.20.
252. An. 2.3.21 ff.
253. An. 2.5.3–15.
254. An. 2.6.6.
255. An. 3.1.2: 10,000 stadia is 1,800 km.
256. An. 2.1.12.
257. An. 3.1.11:
258. cf. An. 4.3.8
259. cf. Lendle 1995, 151.
260. An. 3.1.13 f.
261. An. 3.1.10
262. Lendle 1995, 152.
263. Lendle 1995, 152 f.
264. The Persians had, among other things, an excellent messaging system. Wiesehöfer 1994, 115 ff. Her. 8.98: The mounted Persian messengers are the fastest in the world.
265. cf. An. 3.1.15–25.
266. An. 3.1.47
267. An. 3.2.9.
268. cf. Lendle 1995, 159 f.
269. An. 3.2.10–39.
270. Hans-Joachim Diesner: 'Das Söldnerproblem im alten Griechenland' [The Mercenary Problem in Ancient Greece], in: *Das Altertum* [Antiquity] 3, 1957, 4, 213–223.
271. An. 3.1.4.
272. The Carduchoi are the ancestors of the modern-day Kurds.
273. An. 4.3.2
274. An. 4.7.19.
275. Th's anthropological sketch can be found in the form of *Pathology* in his historical work. 3.82 f. cf. Herwig Görgemanns 1977, 64–93. cf. also Karl Büchner: Sallust, Heidelberg 1982, 334 f.
276. Th. 3.82.2.
277. After thorough discussion of all the available evidence, Breitenbach 1966, 1639–1644 places the writing of An. in the 80s the fourth century, when Xen. was living in Skillus (between 390 BC and 371 BC).

278. Th. 1.75.3. cf. Görgemanns 1977.
279. The Ten Thousand set off from Sardis in March 401 BC. The Battle of Cunaxa occurred in September 401 BC. The Ten Thousand reached Trebizond on the Black Sea in May 400 BC. The entire operation, from Sardis to Trebizond, lasted 15 months. In October 400 BC, the Ten Thousand arrived in Byzantium. In March 399 BC, Xen. handed over command of the 5,000 remaining mercenaries to the Spartan Thibron.
280. An. 4.7.21.
281. Römisch 1972, 65–84, esp. 76–79.
282. James Joyce: *Ulysses* (1922), London 1963, 3, cites Xen.'s 'Thalatta! Thalatta!': 'She is our great sweet mother' – in his poem 'North Sea' in his collection *Travel Scenes*, Heinrich Heine presents Xen.'s An. 4.7 as a motto. In the second section of 'North Sea', Heine begins the poem 'Salutation to the Sea' (1826) with Xen's cry of 'Thalatta! Thalatta!' cf. Rainer Nickel *Die Berühmten Griechische Schriftsteller* [The Famous Greek Authors], Mainz 2010, 164–174.
283. Römisch 1972, 78. Plutarch reports in his biography of Artaxerxes (ch. 20) that the followers of Cyrus happily returned home.
284. *Odyssey* 13.73–92.
285. Manfred Lossau: 'Xenophon's Odyssee', in: *Antike & Abendland* [Antiquity & Occident] 36, 1990, 47–52.
286. An. 4.7.21–26.
287. As later understood by Diodorus 14.29.4.
288. An. 7.1.25–31: Xen's speech to the soldiers.
289. An. 7.8.2.
290. Xen. describes the negotiations with Seuthes in An. 7.2.17–7.3.2.
291. An. 7.8.8.
292. An. 7.8.14 f.
293. An. 7.8.20–23.
294. An. 7.8.23 f.; Hell. 3.1.6.
295. Hell. 3.2.7.
296. Hell. 3.4.20. Herippidas led the followers of Cyrus on the side of the Lacedaemonians in the Battle of Coronea in 394 BC against the Boeotians, Athenians, and others: Hell. 4.3.15.
297. An. 5.3.6.
298. Hell. 4.3.15–20.
299. Hell. 4.3.17.

Bibliography

Bengtson, H.: *Griechische Geschichte von den Anfängen bis in die römische Kaiserzeit* [Greek History from its Origins to the Roman Empire], Munich 1965.

Berve, H.: *Die Tyrannis bei den Griechen* [The Tyranny in Greece], Munich 1967.

Bleckmann, B.: *Der peloponnesische Krieg* [The Peloponnesian War], Munich 2007.

Breitenbach, H. R.: *Xenophon von Athen* [Xenophon of Athens], Stuttgart 1966 (= RE 9 A 2, 1966, 1569–1928).

Broemser, F.: Größe und Niedergang im Geschichtswerk des Thukydides [Size and Decline in the Historical Work of Thucydides], in: *Der altsprachliche Unterricht* [The Classical Language Lesson] 9, 3, 1966, 30–71.

Bruns, I.: *Das literarische Porträt der Griechen im fünften und vierten Jahrhundert vor Christi-Geburt* [The Literary Portrait of the Greeks in the Fifth and Fourth Centuries BC], Berlin 1896.

Canfora, L.: *Die verlorene Geschichte des Thukydides* [The Lost History of Thucydides], Berlin 1990.

Diesner, H.-J.: 'Das Söldnerproblem im alten Griechenland' [The Mercenary Problem in Ancient Greece], in: *Das Altertum* [Antiquity] 3, 1957, 4, 213–223.

Fox, R. L.: *Die klassische Welt. Eine Weltgeschichte von Homer bis Hadrian* [The Classical World. A History of the World from Homer to Hadrian], Stuttgart 2010.

Görgemanns, H.: 'Macht und Moral. Thukydides und die Psychologie der Macht' [Power and Morality. Thucydides and the Psychology of Power], in: *Humanistische Bildung* [Humanist Education] 1/1977, 64–93.

Heubeck, A.: 'Gedanken zu Thukydides' [Thoughts on Thucydides], in: F. Hörmann (ed.): *Die alten Sprachen im Gymnasium* [Ancient Languages at Grammar School], Munich 1957, 115–129.

Jacob, A.: 'Thukydides-Lektüre als Beitrag zur politischen Bildung. Interpretationen zur Pathologie und zur Vorgeschichte der sizilischen Expedition' [Thucydides' Writings as a Contribution to Political Education. Interpretations of the Pathology and History of the Sicilian Expedition], in: *AU* 9, 3, 1966, 72–98.

Jaeger, W.: *Paideia. Die Formung des griechischen Menschen* [Paideia. The Formation of the Greek People], Berlin 1959, Vol. 1, 479–513.

Kaiser, W. B.: 'Zur Anabasislektüre' [Reading Anabasis], in: *AU* 3, 3, 1957, 37–51.

Klauk, E.: 'Die Charakteristiken des Klearchos, Proxenus und Menon in Xenophons Anabasis' [The Characteristics of Clearchus, Proxenus and Menon in Xenophon's Anabasis] (II 6, 1–29), in: *AU* 10, 3, 1967, 21–39.

Klinz, A.: 'Das Methodenkapitel des Thukydides (I 21 ff.). Ein Beitrag zur Behandlung in der Schule' [Thucydides' Methods Chapter (I 21 ff.). A Contribution to Treatment in School], in: *AU* 9, 3, 1966, 99–109.

Landmann, G. P.: *Thukydides. Geschichte des Peloponnesischen Krieges* [Thucydides. History of the Peloponnesian War], Zürich/Stuttgart 1960 and Hamburg 1962 (Rowohlts Klassiker).

Lendle, O.: 'Der Bericht Xenophons über die Schlacht von Kunaxa' [Xenophon's Report on the Battle of Cunaxa], in: *Gymnasium* 13, 1966, 429–452.

Lendle, O.: 'Der Marsch der „Zehntausend' durch das Land der Karduchen' [The March of the 'Ten Thousand' through the Land of the Carduchoi] (Xenophon, Anabasis IV 1. 5–3. 34), in: *Gymnasium* 91, 1984, 202–236.

Lendle, O.: *Kommentar zu Xenophons Anabasis* (Bücher 1–7) [Commentary on Xenophon's Anabasis (Books 1–7)], Darmstadt 1995.

Lesky, A.: *Geschichte der griechischen Literatur* [History of Greek Literature], Bern/ Munich 1971, 512–544.

Lossau, M.: 'Xenophons Odyssee' [Xenophon's Odyssey], in: *Antike & Abendland* [Antiquity & Occident] 36, 1990, 47–52.

Lotze, D.: *Lysander und der Peloponnesische Krieg* [Lysander and the Peloponnesian War], Berlin 1964.

Luschnat, O.: *Thukydides der Historiker* [Thucydides the Historian], Stuttgart 1971 (= RE 12, 1970,

Malitz, J.: 'Sokrates im Athen der Nachkriegszeit (404–399 v. Chr.)' [Socraties in Post-War Athens(404–399 BC)], in: H. Kessler (ed.): *Socrates. Geschichte, Legende, Spiegelungen. Sokrates-Studien II* [Socrates. History. Legend. Reflections. Studying Socrates II], Kusterdingen 1995, 11–38.

Meier, C.: *Athen. Ein Neubeginn der Weltgeschichte* [Athens. A New Beginning to World History], Munich 2004.

Mueller-Goldingen, C.: *Xenophon. Philosophie und Geschichte* [Xenophon. Philosophy and History], Darmstadt 2007.

Reinhardt, K.: 'Thukydides und Machiavelli' [Thucydides and Machiavelli] (1943), in: *Die Krise des Helden. Beiträge zur Literatur- und Geistesgeschichte* [The Crisis of the Hero. Contributions to the Literary and Intellectual History], Munich 1962, 12–88.

Römisch, E.: 'Xenophon', in: E. R. (ed.): *Griechisch in der Schule. Didaktik, Plan und Deutung* [Greek in School. Didactics, Planning and Interpretation], Frankfurt 1972, 65–84.

Schulz, R.: *Athen und Sparta* [Athens and Sparta]. Darmstadt 2005.

Sonnabend, H.: *Thukydides* [Thucydides], Hildesheim 2004.

Taeger, F.: *Das Altertum. Geschichte und Gestalt der Mittelmeerwelt* [Antiquity. History and Shape of the Mediterranean World], Stuttgart 1939 (Study edition of the 6th edition, undated).

Trümpner, H.: 'Klearchos, Militarist oder Soldat? Ein Beitrag zur Politischen Gemeinschaftskunde' [Clearchus, Militarist or Soldier? A Contribution to Political Social Studies], in: *AU* 10, 3, 1967, 5–20.

Weber, G., in: K. Brodersen (ed.): *Virtuelle Antike. Wendepunkte der Alten Geschichte* [Virtual Antiquity. Turning point of Ancient History], Darmstadt 2000, 11–23.

Welwei, K.-W.: *Das klassische Athen. Demokratie und Machtpolitik im 5. und 4.*

Jahrhundert [Classical Athens. Democracy and the Politics of Power in the Fifth and Fourth Centuries], Darmstadt 1999, 247–257.

Werner, H.: 'Griechische Plastik im Unterricht' [Greek Statuary in the Classroom], in: *AU* 20, 3, 1977, 5–27.

Wiesehöfer, J.: *Das antike Persien Von 550 v. Chr. bis 650 n. Chr.* [The Ancient Persians. From 550 BC to 650 AD], München/Zürich 1994.

Index of Names and Terms